Also by Ruby Gwin
A Day That Would End Tearing at Your Heart
The 250th Field Artillery Men Remember World War
World War II
Walter Irvin's Diary: WWI Pharmacist Mate

1st Lt. Raymond Miller Pilot

B-17G Flying Fortress WWII

❦

Ruby Gwin

To My Friend Cheryl:
Please accept this book as a token of my gratitude for what you do for us.
God Bless You and thanks.
Ray Miller

Order this book online at www.trafford.com
or email orders@trafford.com

Most Trafford titles are also available at major online book retailers.

© Copyright 2013 Ruby Gwin.
All rights reserved. No part of this publication may be reproduced, stored in a retrieval system, or transmitted, in any form or by any means, electronic, mechanical, photocopying, recording, or otherwise, without the written prior permission of the author.

Cover design: Ruby Gwin
Book design: Ruby Gwin

Printed in the United States of America.

ISBN: 978-1-4907-1816-3 (sc)
ISBN: 978-1-4907-1817-0 (hc)
ISBN: 978-1-4907-1815-6 (e)

Library of Congress Control Number: 2013919654

Because of the dynamic nature of the Internet, any web addresses or links contained in this book may have changed since publication and may no longer be valid. The views expressed in this work are solely those of the author and do not necessarily reflect the views of the publisher, and the publisher hereby disclaims any responsibility for them.

Any people depicted in stock imagery provided by Thinkstock are models, and such images are being used for illustrative purposes only.
Certain stock imagery © Thinkstock.

Trafford rev. 11/18/2013

www.trafford.com
North America & international
toll-free: 1 888 232 4444 (USA & Canada)
fax: 812 355 4082

For Russell and Richard Miller

Acknowledgments

Any endeavor, such as attempting to author a true story, is really the result of invaluable input from the main source. It has been through Raymond Miller's own vision and enthusiasm in bringing his book into being. His memory has been impeccable during a time in history when he volunteered to serve his country. Very *special* thanks to Raymond's daughter and son, Linda Miller Moorman and Mark Miller, who have been most helpful with the pictures used for their father's book. To Pamela "Davis" Ragan, thanks for her father and sons' stories and pictures. Thanks to Raymond's dear friend, bombardier Harold "Hal" Kristal, whose contribution has been most beneficial. He was frank, forthcoming, and informative. Thanks to Carolyn "Cally" Boatwright, secretary of the 452nd Group; she supplied pictures, etc., of the Deopham Green Air Base where her father was one of the owners of the property where the air base was built in 1942. She has followed the 452nd throughout from her young youth. Thanks to Roann Keller and photographer, David Fraley, for pictures. Special thanks to James "Jim" Debth who was especially helpful with sharing some of his 728th mission experiences and providing many of the B-17 pictures for Raymond's book. Each one's assistance has been invaluable to the author. Raymond's book would not have been possible without each.

Author's photo on cover back by Victoria Barkhart

To my *special* publishing team at Trafford Publishing whom I can't praise enough—many, many thanks.

Heidi Morgan, check-in coordinator
Joel Berou, publishing consultant
Ryan Gavini, marketing consultant
Nick Arden, publishing services associate
John Cain, marketing service representative
James Calonia, manuscript services representative

Introduction

It was on young 1st Lt. Raymond Miller's second mission when he suffered a serious injury as flak fragments penetrated his throat and shattered his breastbone. At twenty-seven-thousand-feet altitude, Raymond was just ninety seconds from unconsciousness and then death. The crew chief climbed through the turret and saw Raymond's oxygen tube had been cut. He put his mask on Raymond while he searched the plane for a walk-around oxygen bottle, which he found at bombs away.

On December 7, 1941, Raymond Miller was playing basketball at the Marion, Indiana, armory, but not until his return home that evening did he learn of the Japanese navy surprise attack on the United States fleet at Pearl Harbor. The preemptive strike was seen as essential to hamper United States defense efforts. The Japanese audacious attack on that beautiful day under sunny Hawaiian sky led to the United States entry into World War II in both the Pacific and European theaters. It was then it became apparent to Raymond that he'd have to go into the armed services.

After Raymond completed his primary flight training and basic and advanced training of Air Corps pilots, he received his commission in the Army Air Forces. In May 1944, he went to an overseas training unit. After completion of his overseas training, he was sent to an air base near a little village called Deopham Green, near Norwich, England. It was here that Raymond was assigned to the United States Army Air Corps, 452nd Bombardment Group (Heavy), 8th Army Air

Force, 728 Bombing Squadron activated 1 January 1943. In addition to strategic missions, the air force supported ground forces and carried out interdictory operations over hostile territory.

Raymond copiloted the United States Army's Eighth Air Force B-17G bomber, the Flying Fortress. The Boeing Flying Fortress, the United States heavy bomber, was operational all through the war. To provide a combined around-the-clock bomber offensive against Germany and occupied Europe the United States Air Forces spearheaded the daylight raids and the Royal Air Force spearheaded the night raids.

Raymond's second mission November 5, 1944, was a *No Milk Run,* or little or no danger. The crew was scheduled to go to Ludwigshafen on the Rhine River. As they neared the target and turned on what they call the IP, the initial point, they made a forty-mile bomb run down the target. The flak was very intense.

Raymond critically injured and spent some time in a hospital in England. It would be late December before Raymond resumed flying on another mission. Raymond would go on and fly twenty more missions over Europe. The B-17 Flying Fortress with P-51 Mustang fighter escort in the skies was the icon of the Eighth Air Force as they faced the Nazis during World War II.

Raymond Miller was one of those who aspired to face personal risk in serving the nation. It was by choice, due to his innate love of country and spirit of self-sacrifice. He says, "I was just doing my duty."

Only one of three airmen survived the air battle over Europe during World War II, exceeding those of the United States Marine Corps and the United States Navy combined. Raymond's near-death experience never stopped him from carrying on, and he would resume flying on his first target mission to Darmstadt, Germany. To resume flying was a motivation for Raymond. He *never* let fear lead and concentrated on his flying for he knew fear leads to inferior performance. It was what he was trained to do. Not allowing static into the mind, he chose to remain focused in that cockpit. Raymond knew it was exactly where he belonged, flying missions over the flak-filled skies of Nazi Europe.

1st Lt. Raymond Miller Pilot

Many of our United States Air Force men paid a high price for their heroic efforts for victory. It all leaves a mask of riddles, where one wonders—why? Time only deepens the wonder. No one doubts that those who flew those many horrible and necessary missions were with cause. After the audacious attack on the United States fleet at Pearl Harbor, the United States was brought in to a war that our president was trying to avoid.

The only thing new in the world is the history you don't know.

—President Harry S. Truman.

Raymond Miller's story is a penetrating, epic portrait of a young lieutenant warrior and the human expression of war. It is a story that tells the difference between truth and myth, the meaning of being a young copilot in the Army Air Corps-one who had a keen and deep appreciation for the opportunity to serve his country with duty and honor. Raymond Miller's stories don't make the history books of how a pilot and copilot of a B-17 aircraft commanded a crew in aerial offensive operations into perilous zone of danger.

Raymond Miller chose to leave the Purdue University Reserve Officers' Training Corps [ROTC] and his Purdue baseball team with his brother Russell to serve with the United States Army Air Corps (USAAC) USAF. Raymond is a quiet, humble gentleman, spending his later years giving presentations about memories of his bombing missions as a copilot. He is grateful for the opportunity in 2012 to go to Washington DC on a veteran's honor flight (WWII veterans' tribute journey). It was a trip of a lifetime—just another one of the accolades that have been paid to him these last few years.

Raymond Miller's book is an account of the war as he and his comrades experienced it. But it is not about the glorious conquest of the crew in the B-17 Flying Fortress, but words of the B-17 crewmen that flew over enemy targets doing a job they were sent to do. There are some things that Raymond Miller will keep inside. Some things are never spoken—only seen through the eye and felt in the heart.

Chapter 1

A Symbolic Choice

Young Raymond Miller served as copilot, flying in 8th Air Force combat missions over Northern and Central Europe in World War II. Their aircraft was a four-engine heavy bomber known as the B-17 or Flying Fortress. The aircraft was touted as a strategic weapon; it was a potent, high-flying, long-range bomber that was able to defend itself.

After the Pearl Harbor surprise attack in 1941, with the country living under the cloud of war on two war fronts, Raymond, with his brother Russell, symbolically chose to enlist into the reserves on a fall day October 13, 1942. Later, his younger brother Richard would enlist after graduating from Indianapolis, Indiana's John Herron School of Art.

Raymond "Ray" Miller was born in Mount Vernon, Ohio, on October 3, 1922. Raymond was the oldest of three boys. Russell was born on April 20, 1924, and Richard on December 9, 1925. The boys grew up deeply connected, being close in age. They had fun playing, working, and planning things together, with interests in flying.

As children of working-class parents Leroy and Josephine Miller, they were poor. Their father, Leroy, was restless and would move the family from place to place. In 1927, the family would move from Ohio to Marion, Indiana, where his mother's parents, Calvin and Jennie Griffin, were living. His mother was born in a small town southeast of Marion called Jonesboro. Most of the time, to go to school or church it meant walking. Raymond was enrolled in School Number 9 on Salem Pike, about 1 1/2 miles east of his grandpa Griffin's house where the family was staying. With there not being any school bus, Raymond walked or ran to and from school. In the winter, sometimes after running, his lungs would burn from the frigid cold.

Raymond was a good student. He was a natural at whatever he did and not afraid to work hard. With Russell and Richard, he worked on different projects. They each had chores to do. They helped with the garden and cared for the chickens. The three drank three gallons of milk a day. On the Spratt's farm where their mother bought the milk, they helped Mr. Spratt with his chores. They worked helping them to make hay and putting it up in the barn's hayloft. They were not paid, but for the three, it was fun and kept them busy and entertained. They also shucked corn and loaded it on the wagon. To their north was the municipal golf course where they became involved at being caddies. They would go to the caddie house at five o'clock in the morning and wait for jobs. They were fortunate to get some of the regular golf players to pick them to caddy. If they were good and didn't lose any golf balls, they got paid twenty-five cents for every nine holes. If lucky, they went eighteen holes and made fifty cents, and if they didn't lose golf balls, they were tipped another quarter. Sometimes they made as much as one dollar and fifty cents a day. They felt rich for they were making money.

The family moved to Five Points on the northwest side of Marion, and it actually was a place where the roads merged and made five points. Not living in the city limits, Raymond went to the ninth grade at the Marion Sweetzer High School. Raymond tried out for the basketball team, which called for evening practice. Since the school bus had already left, Raymond had to walk home about six miles. He says, needless to say, "I didn't do that very many times, but to play basketball, I had to make that long walk."

While in high school, Raymond got a job at the Marion, Indiana Shoe Factory and was paid 35¢ an hour, $13 a week. Feeling rich with his earned savings, he went downtown to the car agency and bought a 1932 Plymouth for $100. Being proud of his first car purchase, he took his father along for a ride when he went to play ball at Summitville. The car broke down with a flat tire. Raymond, in a change of mind, took the car back downtown to the car dealer who said he'd take the Plymouth in on a trade, so Raymond traded for a 1930 Model A Ford coupe for $90. That car would last Raymond fifteen years until 1954 when he sold it for $120. It provided transportation for his father and Richard, which Raymond was most proud of.

In 1939, Raymond became heavily involved in playing baseball, which pleased his father. He hadn't participated in a whole lot of sports. His major sport was baseball, although he did play on the golf team and played a little football. Raymond graduated from Marion High School in Indiana in 1940. There was a local restaurant called the Hilltop where the young people gathered after games and dances. Raymond would stop at Hilltop Restaurant and listen to all the latest of news.

In school Raymond took science classes and for his merit performance received the Bausch and Lomb Honorary Science Award. Raymond was intelligent. While he was in the sixth grade he was promoted a half grade ahead from class 6-A to class 6-B.

In 1940, Raymond went to work at the Anaconda Wire Factory. During that time, he played a lot of ball. After staying out of school for a year, in 1941, Raymond enrolled in Marion College, and in the spring of that year, he traveled to Greenville, Tennessee, and tried out for a class D professional baseball team. To his amazement, his father let him and Russell use his new 1939 Plymouth Chrysler to drive to Tennessee. Raymond tried out and made the club. He joined the team at the end of the school term. After some time, he received word from Greenville that the league was folding because of the war and there was no transportation.

Raymond was at the Marion Armory playing basketball on December 7, 1941. When Raymond got home, they received news that Pearl Harbor had been attacked by the Japanese. The next day, President Roosevelt stood before Congress and called to America to fight. He called December 7 a "date which will live in infamy."

Congress declared war against Japan. At the time, Raymond's father thought that he was the one who was going to have to go into the service. The next week, young men flocked to volunteer because of the shock and carnage of the Japanese's surprise attack. The Selective Service Act ratified in 1940 was better known as the Selected Training and Service Act. The United States Navy and the Marine Corps did not participate in conscription. The conscript swelled the ranks of the United States Army. In one month, sixty thousand men had enlisted in the United States Army and Navy.

When Raymond's father found out that it may be his sons who would be going into the military, he suggested that he take them down to the Everglades and hide out. "Well," Raymond says, "you can imagine our reaction. We refused to do that."

Russell graduated from high school in 1941. In the fall of 1942, Raymond and Russell enrolled in Purdue University, West Lafayette, Indiana. On October 13, 1942, they walked across the West Lafayette Bridge to the recruiters' office in Lafayette, Indiana and enlisted in the Reserve Army Air Corps. This allowed them to keep attending school and be available if they were needed. Raymond had gone to Purdue University majoring in civil engineering. He was to play on the baseball team in the spring, and during the winter, he cleaned the locker room and was given all his meals free at the student union. In those days, it was known as a scholarship-type token, just at a totally different scale than today. Purdue began to give out scholarships in 1958. Raymond and Russell stayed at a rooming house where there were bunk beds. They traveled home every weekend in Raymond's old Model A Ford. They enjoyed their time while attending Purdue University.

Chapter 2

Called to Serve

Raymond and Russell both were called into the service in the spring of 1943. They reported to Fort Thomas, Kentucky. They arrived there in the evening, and they were very hungry. The mess hall was closed, and all they had left was spinach. Though never liking spinach much, they ate it. It was there that they sent their clothing, all covered with soot and smoke, back to their mother and Raymond says, "Poor mother cried at the thought of us being on the train and being called into service."

After the United States' entry into war after the Pearl Harbor attack, the number of volunteers for the pilot training was enormous. Training came in five stages to accommodate the large number of volunteers. The previous four stages were extended to the five stages with the creation of the preflight stage in 1942.

Raymond and Russell, for basic training, were sent to Biloxi, Mississippi, where they would stay together, and then they were sent to ground school in San Antonio, Texas. From there, they went to college training at Jefferson College, in Saint Louis, Missouri, where they continued their studies in navigation, Morse code, engine maintenance, and celestial navigation, as well as learning the basic education that was needed. All pilots in cadet school were taught code and had to receive and send at least twenty words a minute to be able to graduate.

While in Saint Louis, their parents visited them. It was extremely hot, and their father told them he had to drive less than the fifty-mile speed limit, not because of the speed limit, but because the tires on the car were almost bald, and he didn't dare drive faster for fear of a blowout. New tires were not available because rubber was on the war priority list, so their father put two old tires in the trunk in case they were needed. This makes Raymond recall the time he bought new tires for his 1930 Model A Ford, and his father, angrily, asked, "What are you buying tires for?"

Those new tires that Raymond put on his Model A Ford turned out to be a profitable purchase because with rubber rationed during the war, tires were hard to get. The tires lasted on the car during the whole ensuing war.

While assigned in Saint Louis, Raymond was fortunate enough to see a baseball game between the Saint Louis Browns and the New York Yankees and got to see his hero, Bill Dickey the catcher, which was always Raymond's favorite position. The game was played at the old Sportsman Park. Today, it is the site of the Herbert Hoover Boy's Club. A baseball field is at the same location where the Cardinals and the Browns once played.

Russell played baseball until he broke his arm and lost his chance to be a pitcher. Baseball was a natural interest for the boys as it was for their father. Their father, a good baseball player, played for the Twilight League. He was gifted with being able to pitch with either his right or left hand.

Raymond and Russell spent six months at the college training detachment at Saint Louis, Missouri. They had ten-hour dual flying in a piper cub to see if they could fly or not. There was never a shortage of young volunteers for air cadet training for there was prestige being a young cadet.

From there they were sent to *primary flight training* in Tulsa, Oklahoma, in January 1944, where they flew an open-cockpit PT-19 Fairchild single-engine model plane with a 120-horsepower engine. They hand cranked the engine to get it started. It was a low-wing plane with a double cockpit where the student and instructor would ride. It was there that they learned to do acrobatics, slow rolls, snap rolls, and split Ss. They learned to shoot landings and do cross-country flying and were taught how to fly solo. Raymond says, "You had to learn to take off and land after six hours. You can imagine how tense I was when the instructor climbed out and told me, 'Take the plane around and land three times.' Talk about being frightened! There was one student who went up with an instructor doing acrobatics and the wing had come off. The only way we could converse with one another was through a speaking tube. The instructor tried to tell the student to bail out and banged on everything, but the student froze and couldn't move. Finally, the instructor bailed out, and of all things, the plane went upside down, and the student was thrown clear. Both the instructor and student were safe. The acrobatics, I think, were possibly done to see if you got sick. If you did, flying was not for you."

They attended ground school and physical training as part of their training as well. Raymond said, "I got lost during my solo flight at Tulsa while in my primary training. I tried to find the landmarks, railroad tracks, and buildings—I never had the sense to read a depot sign, which was something they never taught. In the process of flying, I looked around and saw a glimpse in the sky—kind of like a silver glimpse—and thought, *Well, it won't hurt to fly toward those.* And sure enough they were airliners for the Tulsa Municipal Airport. I felt I had no other recourse but to land at the airport. At random, I called the instructor and thought, *Well, this is no more for me.* He had me to fly formation back with him. He never washed me out."

During their primary training, the instructors were middle-aged civilians who had hundreds and thousands of hours of experience. They were fortunate, for the instructors taught those things only an experienced trainer could do. For example: they had very little auxiliary fields and short runs or strips to get in on—they couldn't come in and make a gradual approach. They taught them to sideslip and lose elevation quickly just before landing. These were things only an experienced trainer could teach. The trainees were grateful to have such superb training.

It was at Tulsa that Russell washed out of flying training. Raymond felt sorry for him. His instructor told Russell that he would make a good Sunday-afternoon pilot, but he had no sense of direction. Tulsa is where Raymond and Russell would part ways. Raymond and Russell would be separated after being together since their entry into the Army Air Corps. This was where they would lose track of one another. They didn't see one another until after the war. Russell went on to gunner school in Colorado. Raymond went on to *basic training* at Coffeyville, Kansas, and there he flew the basic trainer called a Vultee BT-13 Valiant. There they learned to fly at night, make night landings, and make cross-country flights. The BT-13 was a larger low-wing model plane with a 450-horsepower engine. It had variable pitch propeller and no retractable landing gear, but it had a huge engine that they didn't have (at least for those days), so cadets were very much impressed by the plane.

While in basic training, cadets had military instructors. Raymond said, "Not that I am intelligent, but I was flying with an instructor to an auxiliary field, and on our approach, we couldn't touch down. We would overshoot every time, and I thought, *Hey, something is wrong.* I said, 'Why don't we turn and come in 180 degrees from the other way? I think we are landing downwind.' This was at night when we couldn't see the wind sock. The instructor didn't know we were landing downwind, so we turned around and came in the other way and made it. That was not a reflection of my knowledge, just a stroke of luck, but the point is, some of those military instructors weren't too good."

From Kansas, Raymond went to *advanced flying training* in Pampa, Texas, in May 1944 and learned to fly what was called an AT-17 Cessna Bobcat (which pilots called the Bamboo Bomber) twin-engine advanced-trainer aircraft, sometimes referred to as a UC-78. With their instructor, they learned dead reckoning, cross-country flying, and shooting landings. That particular stretch of country was always plagued by huge wind gusts, and sometimes, they would have to land in a fifty-mile-per-hour wind and crosswinds. Many times, they had to come in at full throttle so they could get back on the ground. Raymond says, "I had quite an education there in instrument flying and some formation flying, cross-country. At night, we flew airways that were lit by beacons. They were ten miles apart, and we learned to fly on the radio range for our navigation."

The students were sent on a rendezvous mission with an instructor, taking off from different places. They had no other information except they were to rendezvous at a certain point. Raymond was command pilot with a copilot. The copilot evidently thought they were gaining too much and he lowered the flaps and they did not come up. Raymond had to search for an auxiliary field overlay and found a farm field and landed there. Raymond sent the copilot to call the instructor who brought a mechanic and got the flaps up. The instructor told Raymond to fly formation with him back to the base. Raymond thought that was the end of his flight career, but the instructor must have known the situation because when they landed, he winked at Raymond and said, "Go on to where you stay."

The three stages—primary, basic, and advanced—were the common training of all Air Corps pilots, and then upon graduation from advanced, students received their wings and bars. The new pilots were given additional periods of specialized instructions suited to their military assignments. Their transition flying period was applied generally to a pilot learning to operate an unfamiliar plane. After a pilot had earned his wings, he found transition to combat planes was a more difficult undertaking than transitions to training planes. It involved learning to fly a complex, high-performance aircraft but also the acquisition of flying techniques preliminary to operational unit training. Transition was an adequate stage in the major pilot programs. Raymond found his advance instructor to be cruel—"put you through the mill and never gave you any limitation." Raymond thought to himself, *If I ever meet you after I get out of here . . . !*

Once, looking back, Raymond realized that the instructor's job was to try to prepare his cadets with self-discipline that would help protect them when called to use one's abilities or resources or when making decisions when challenged. It was the same drills that they had known.

From Pampa, Texas, Raymond went on an *overseas training unit* in Ardmore, Oklahoma, where he was given the choice of going into four-engine training in a chosen aircraft or to take overseas training. While at Ardmore, they were never actually taught forced landings, but the pilot was made aware that he should familiarize himself with ditching procedures before taking off on a long over-water flight or putting the plane down safely on terrain. Gene Autry had a ranch at Ardmore, Oklahoma, that he donated to the Army Air Corps. The lake could be used to simulate water landings. The wide wings of the B-17 helped the airplane to stay afloat after being ditched on the water. It gave the crew two minutes to get their inflated raft and get out of the plane before it sank. Forced landing on water, flat land, and on rugged terrain involved considerable skill for a pilot.

Raymond was asked if he wanted to stay four more months and fly a four-engine aircraft, but he chose overseas training where he learned to be copilot on the B-17 Flying Fortress. While training, Raymond was able to resume playing with a softball team. Being a baseball player, he got to play baseball with Del Wilbur, a scrappy major league catcher, and Enos Slaughter, nicknamed Country, who batted left-handed and threw right-handed. It was quite a treat for Raymond. Wilbur and Slaughter played for the Cardinals. Del Wilbur entered the military service in 1942. In 1943, he graduated from officer candidate school as a lieutenant and was assigned as a physical instructor at San Antonio Aviation Cadet Center in Texas, where he managed the baseball team.

Raymond's team entered the Southwest Regional Softball Tournament and won the entire southwest championship and was scheduled to go to Cleveland, Ohio, for the National Softball Finals. With Raymond going overseas, an arrangement was made by the air force through the auspices of the Red Cross for Raymond, Russell, and Richard to come home at the same time. Unfortunately, the date overlapped with the National Softball Tournament so Raymond forwent the tournament in favor of being home with the family.

They had finished their training and were ready to go overseas in September 1944. In October of 1944, Raymond's crew, nineteen-and twenty-year-old boys, were assigned to go to Lincoln, Nebraska, to pick up an airplane valued at $400,000 at the time. From there, they ferried the B-17 across to Grenier Air Force Base, New Hampshire, stayed overnight, and from there to Goose Bay, Labrador, where they stayed again overnight. With it being very cold, they had to build tents around their engines and set heaters below to keep the engines warm. From Goose Bay, they flew to Iceland. The radio operator was very apprehensive because he thought he would have to use celestial navigation to get across the Atlantic Ocean. At higher elevations, ice began to form on their wings and propellers, and they couldn't descend because of the altitude of the mountains in Greenland. With the altitude being ten thousand feet high, they had to stay well above and rev up the engines to throw the ice off the propellers.

Since they were flying at a higher altitude, the pilot instructed the crew in the radio room to go on oxygen. For some reason or other, they never obeyed the order. On the intercom checks they began to hear some foolish replies to their question. Raymond, assigned as the medical officer, went back to check and found that the radio room crew had not put on their oxygen masks and were suffering from the effects of anoxia. Raymond managed to put masks on their faces, and they each recovered. Upon their landing in Iceland, it was very cold, and as in Goose Bay, Labrador, they built tents over the engines again and placed heaters below.

They landed in the eastern part of England at Valley, Wales. It was raining. The English sent a truck (which is called lorry in British English) driver to drive them to their base. The driver went by a pub and said, "Teatime!"

The driver stopped the truck and went in and got his tea and left them sitting out in the rain. Upon arriving at the base, the crewmen were greeted by a radio broadcast from Germany. "We know you have arrived in Valley, Wales, and we are ready to greet you," then naming their airplane, naming the crewmen, their ranking, their serial numbers, describing their destination, and saying *"What goes up comes down."* German espionage was very efficient.

From Valley, Wales, they were assigned to an air base near a little village called Deopham Green (pronounced [defam]), near Norwich on the eastern side of England, which gave them a little more head start when they went on their missions. They were closer to the continent of Europe, much closer than being on the western side of the Atlantic.

At Deopham Green, they spent a few days of practice missions getting acquainted with the area. If they had clear weather for takeoff, a front came through in the wintertime about every four hours, and they had to expect to come down through the clouds when they returned vice versa. One night, they climbed above the clouds and there was a perfect moonlight. Raymond says, "The most beautiful sight I ever seen in my life."

Infant Raymond Miller.

1st Lt. Raymond Miller Pilot

L-R: Raymond, Richard, and Russell Miller standing with a large kite that their father had made.

L-R: Richard, Raymond, and Russell Miller standing next to their father's new 1938 Chrysler.

Raymond Miller with books in hand,
headed out for high school.

Raymond Miller handsomely dressed in a suit, standing in
front of his 1930 Model A Ford coupe in 1939.

1st Lt. Raymond Miller Pilot

Raymond Miller's Marion, Indiana, high school graduation picture in 1940.

Raymond Miller in his ROTC suit.

L-R: Raymond and Russell Miller dressed in their ROTC clothing. They were going to Purdue University in Lafayette, Indiana (1942).

Raymond and Russell's parents visited during basic training at Saint Louis, Missouri. *L-R*: Russell, Leroy and Josephine "Josie" Miller, Raymond, and longtime neighbor, Dave Shelley.

1st Lt. Raymond Miller Pilot

Raymond Miller's Army Air Corps photo.

Raymond Miller in primary flight training in Tulsa, Oklahoma, where he flew a PT-19 Fairchild airplane.

Chapter 3

First Mission

As part of the general military expansion after the surprise attack on Pearl Harbor, extensive programs were constituted. The USAAF joined the battle in 1942. The 452nd Bombardment Group (Heavy) was established on 14 May 1943 and activated on 6 June 1943. The crews were trained with B-17s. On 5 February 1944, the 452nd Bombardment Group entered combat. From that date until April 1945, 250 combat missions were flown with the loss of 186 B-17s. The 452nd Bomb Group was assigned to Deopham Green Airbase and consisted of four squadrons, the 728th, 729th, 730th, and 731th. The group was in the 45th Wing, the 3rd Division, and 8th Air Force. Their insignia was a square *L*.

On 20 October 1944, the following names were assigned to 452nd Bomb Group and spent a part of October doing practice missions, instrument flying, and night flying to get prepared for their stint in combat. At that time, they were given their rank: pilot, 1st Lt. Harry F. Simmons; copilot, 2nd Lt. Raymond Miller; navigator, 2nd Lt. John F. Nortness; bombardier/flight officer, Harold Kristal; Cpl. Roger Boman; Cpl. Lynn M. Davis Jr.; Cpl. George Culnon; Cpl. Donald J. McHugh; Cpl. Donald E. Sutter; and Cpl. Raymond W. Bromps.

Once the practices for combat missions were finished and the crew was ready for combat, their ranks were changed: 2nd Lt. Harold Kristal, bombardier; T/Sgt. Lynn M. Davis, engineer-gunner; S/Sgt. Roger L. Boman, ball turret; S/Sgt. Donald McHugh, waist gunner, S/Sgt. Ray W. Bromps, tail gunner. Cpl. Donald E. Sutter checked out.

When the new crew arrived at the air base, the pilot and copilot were not experienced, so they were assigned to fly two missions with an experienced crew. On November 3, 1944, 1st Lt. Harry F. Simmons flew to Merseburg, Germany, with a veteran crew. This was a very difficult mission. It was where young men would get a first taste of war they would never forget. Many would pay a high price for their heroic efforts for victory. The target was the Leuna refinery. The Germans had twice the number of antiaircraft guns placed there than at Berlin. They had been brought there to protect their dwindling petroleum supply. There were twenty-three air raids made over the Merseburg synthetic oil refineries corridor, a place that took its toll on the air crewmen and their machinery. It was known that airmen dreaded Merseburg more than Ludwigshafen, Berlin, Hamburg, Munich, and Kassel.

The next day, November 4, 2nd Lt. Raymond Miller was assigned to fly with 2nd Lt. Rasimer Traynelis and a crew on an easy mission and saw a few bursts of flak. Raymond, not seeing flak before, turned to the pilot and asked, "Is that flak?" The pilot responded, "Yes."

The enemy had very inaccurate flak and only one fighter came through to attack, so it was what was called a milk run. It was customary for the pilot to fly to the target and for the copilot to fly the return leg back to the base. The copilot, as a chief assistant, must be able to take over and act in the place of the pilot at any time.

The 452nd Bomb Group was just one of the twenty-four B-17 heavy bomber groups that became stationed in England as part of the United States Army's Eighth Air Force. In addition to the B-17 heavy groups, four medium bomber groups, twenty fighter groups, and nineteen B-24 heavy bomber groups were assigned to the Mighty Eighth Air Forces in England. The Deopham Green Airfield was constructed in 1942-1943. It comprised of a 2,000-yard runway, two 1,400-yard auxiliary runways, a perimeter track, fifty-one hardstands (forty-nine loops, virtually all spectacles) and two hand pans, and two hangars located to the north and southwest. Lying to the west was the temporary camp that accommodated 2,900 personnel. On the airbase were sixty B-17s divided into four squadrons, and each squadron consisted of nine to twelve aircraft. On a bombing mission, there were usually three squadrons assigned to go on a mission, which meant that a group flying a bombardier mission might number twenty-seven to thirty-six B-17s. Each B-17 squadron had a crew of ten. That was changed when it was decided that there was no need for two waist gunners. The first mission of the 452nd was on February 5, 1944, and their targeting was to Romilly, France.

The three squadrons to fly were lead, high, and low squadron. Nine to twelve aircraft assigned to each squadron on a bomb mission. They would disperse, and the lead squadron would turn at what they called the initial point and fly on ahead. The high squadron then would follow along, going over the target, and the low squadron followed last. They were the lowest of the aircraft group and the most vulnerable, for the enemy gunner always shot and used their shells to explode below their aircraft. When they exploded, the shrapnel would spread out like a shotgun and all those fragments would come rushing up from underneath. They always shot low so the low element of the squadron was involved most heavily with the flak gunners.

At the start of the bomb run, the bombardier would take over the aircraft with his bomb sight and controlled the aircraft as they went down the bomb run. The gunners would be at their station to repel enemy aircraft and also report flak and what was coming in. If they could take any evasive action whatsoever, they would try to do that. After dropping the bombs over the target, the pilots would take back control of the aircraft and make a sharp turn, pick up lot of speed and regroup (rally together) for the flight back home. They did that without the bomb loads and much less fuel so they could increase their airspeed and try to get home much quicker. The 452nd Bomb Group would be among the last of the B-17 heavy bomber groups to arrive in England. The timing of its arrival would later prove to be at a critical time in the war's history.

Chapter 4

Second Mission

The following day, November 5, 1944, was No Milk Run. Raymond was assigned to go to Ludwigshafen, located across the Rhine River from Mannheim. It was two cities on each side of the river, like Minneapolis and Saint Paul in the United States. Ludwigshafen was an industrial city and home of chemical giant BASF. Mannheim was an important supplier of parts for German planes—this being a prime target for the Allied bomber command.

Raymond rode copilot with veteran pilot Lt. Allen Hamman and his crew on B-17G *That's All Jack* for this mission. If you weren't over at the mess hall by 3:00 a.m., the orderly (charge of quarters) would wake those scheduled for a mission. The crewmen quickly dressed and hurried over to mess hall for a hearty breakfast and then adjourned to the intelligence section where mission details were kept top secret until the curtain was pulled back from the map, and then you learned your target for that day.

During the night, scouts would go out on a weather-reconnaissance mission and gather information, which was most beneficial for the intelligence people. It was a very hazardous mission because a single aircraft flew the mission without any fighter escort. The aircraft crew would scout the course for the combat crews' next day missions, recording temperature, wind drifts at various altitudes, cloud cover, icing conditions—on through a whole weather checklist. The information would be transmitted back to headquarters in code at regular intervals. It would be given to the aircraft crews at the briefing, but its primary use would be in planning the mission—which targets could be hit visually, what the wind would be like, and so on. The instructors would estimate what all they knew about the number of fighters, amount of flak, and guns firing, as well as what the weather would be, at which point the group would assemble, and what the altitude would be. They told how to fly what they believed a flak corridor, where they wouldn't be exposed to flak on the way to target except the battle lines.

If it was a clear day, the Germans in the battle lines could see the B-17s and would fire 88-millimeter antiaircraft guns (88s), concentrating on the squadron leader. They were very accurate with their firing. The intelligence mapped out flak corridors for them to fly through, knowing where the guns were in Germany, and routed the pilots through and made diversionary attacks on other targets to draw the enemy fighters away from the bombers. Raymond says it is amazing just how the intelligence people could put those missions together and have them work so well.

The crews would enter their fueled aircraft after the ordinance people would have loaded with bombs and ammunition. They would have their flight suits, oxygen, and all that they carried on the bomb mission. They would go out to the flight line, come to the runway, and run through a very intense checklist. Once they completed their ground checks, they moved the plane out on the runway in the takeoff position and stand, put the brakes on, and run the engine up with all the power they could get. Then they would take the brakes off and go down the runway and hope to get off with all that tremendous load and fuel. With it being Raymond's first mission with an experienced crew, he watched the engine temperatures and everything he was supposed to do.

They flew a secret altitude no one knew it so when the reference was made to it they would say "Devils three," which meant they would be three thousand feet below the assigned altitude, or "Angels five" that meant they were supposed to go five thousand feet above the secret altitude.

Their assembly point was supposed to be at fifteen thousand feet, so they climbed and climbed over the air base, and when they got there, the fuel gauge had gone half down and they hadn't left England yet. Raymond was very apprehensive, and he nudged the pilot and asked, "Will we make it with fuel?"

The pilot replied, "Oh yes, we'll make it."

Their designated altitude climb was twenty-eight thousand feet. They climbed from their assembly point to their designated point and then started their long, slow climb on their way to targets on the continent, which might take two hours or whatever time it took to climb up twenty-eight thousand feet with the B-17s and B-24s in a thirty-six-plane formation. At that, they would assemble with the entire wing (a group of aircraft) and continue climbing. Each group had its own assigned turf where the group leaders would fly in a circular pattern until the exact minute they needed to join the group in the wing or division. The groups may not have the same target, but each would strike some place in Germany—a ball bearing plant, railway junction, bridge, or something that would keep the German manufactory process disrupted.

As they got near the target and turned on what they call the IP, the initial point, *That's All Jack* made a forty-mile bomb run down to the target. Unlike Raymond's first mission, the flak was close, very intense. Raymond saw one or two burst near him. Some shrapnel shattered the front window, came through, knocked him back, and it hit him in the throat. The pilot was blinded with shattered glass. The crew chief, flight engineer T/Sgt. Joseph M. Botta, climbed through his turret and saw Raymond's oxygen tube had been cut. He put his mask on Raymond then searched the plane for a walk-around oxygen bottle. Luckily, he found it just at bombs away. At twenty-seven-thousand-feet altitude, Raymond had about ninety seconds before he would lose unconsciousness, and then he would die. He was semiconscious but remembers that he had a very powerful feeling of peace that he had never encountered before—a light of unearthly brilliance. His mind seemed to float away from his body. For Raymond, it would have been a peaceful end, "I didn't want to come back to any more killing."

Normal practice was to make a sharp turn, pick up speed, and get out of the flak as quickly as possible. The crew chief grabbed Raymond by the shoulders and tried to pull him out of the seat, thinking it would help. Trying to help, Raymond put his feet up on the control column, and down the plane went. The pilot had glass in his eyes and was not able to see very well. T/Sgt. Joseph M. Botta climbed into the pilot's seat and finished the bomb run and then left the formation to fly the plane back to England. Pilot Allen Hamman had gotten his eyesight back enough to fly the plane, and the B-17 came in for landing, having fired "wounded" flares to indicate wounded onboard, which alerted the waiting ambulance. Lieutenant Hamman would later say, "They had run out of red flares and used green, orange flares—whatever they had."

The bombardier had keep pressure on Raymond's neck injury all during the flight back to base. The waiting ambulance came to pick Raymond up. Raymond spent three hours in the ambulance with a nurse slapping him in the face to keep him awake until they could find a hospital. Once they found a hospital, the required surgery was done.

During the early practice runs and preparation for bombing raids, the top turret gunner was given stick time, when he took control of the plane and learned to land in an emergency situation as on this *No Milk Run* mission. The pilot, flight engineer, bombardier, gunner, and crew had saved Raymond's life. Bombardier 2nd Lt. Amber G. Sutherland IV had been a VMI (twenty-five cadets who pursed a four-year course of study), and Sutherland's chosen course was medical training. Arterial bleeding was under more pressure and moved rapidly, making it hard for clots to form. It was the hardest to deal with. Arterial bleeding called for professional medical help as soon as possible. Lieutenant Sutherland stopped the bleeding and laid Raymond down on the deck below the cabin so he could attend him until they could get him back to the base. The forty degrees below helped to keep the blood from flowing. Lieutenant Sutherland knowing how to stop the bleeding saved Raymond's life.

It would be late December before Raymond was able to go on another mission flight. During his hospital stay, flak hit the crew's airplane engines, and they couldn't make it back to base. The pilot was forced to make a crash landing with the B-17F *Saltine Warrior*. They got back to the England base via Belgium and were issued a brand-new B-17G Fortress airplane named *Warzend*. Raymond never got to fly a mission on the B-17F *Saltine Warrior*. His crew made thirteen run missions while he was in the hospital recuperating. Many times upon their return, they would break the rules and, before landing, would fly over the hospital. The pilot would put the engines in low pitch, which made quite a rumbling noise, and *buzz* the hospital—their way to let him know they were safely back.

On the November 5, 1944, mission, Lieutenant Hamman gave Raymond command of the aircraft for one hour. Sadly, Raymond never got to fly the aircraft back home after the bomb run had been completed.

*Allied bombs hit the city of Ludwigshafen in 121 separate raids during the war. Allied troops advanced reaching Ludwigshafen and Mannheim in March 1945. The infantry entered Mannheim unopposed. Mannheim was an important industrial center for Nazi Germany. There has been a large American Military presence in the area ever since. *Marshalling Yards* is the name the Eighth Air Forces used for railroad yards.

> *Unit history for Ludwigshafen Mission, 5 November 1944 by office of the Intelligence Officer:*
>
> (Unclassified)
>
> 6 November 1944
>
> 1. The 452nd Bomb Group (H) flew lead, High and Low squadrons making up the 45th "A" Group to attack the secondary target or "Marshalling Yards" at Ludwigshafen. Thirty-four (34) plus four (4) PFF A/C were airborne with all attacking except one mechanical abort in the "C" squadron.

2. Due to the coverage over the Primary Target the secondary target was bombed visually. "A" or lead Squadron SAV's show poor results as bombs fell two miles WSW of target. "B" or High squadron SAV's show fair results. "C" or Low squadron SAV's show poor results with center of bomb pattern approx. 4000 ft. South of MPI at junction of South end of Marshalling Yards.
3. Flak on crossing the battle line was meager, inaccurate, and tracking. Over the target flak was accurate, intense, tracking and barrage. Twenty-two aircraft (22) A/C received minor battle damage and four (4) received major from AA. Two personnel were wounded. No E/A were encountered.
4. Difficulties encountered on this mission included:
    (a) Lead PFF equipment failed at (I. P) and deputy led on bomb run.
    (b) Lead A/C of "A" squadron was hit by flak and bombs were released prematurely.
    (c) Fighter support first reported at R.P.

Harold P. Thoreson,
Major, Air Corps,
Intelligence Officer.

Chapter 5

Mission Target

This chapter was handwritten by Raymond Miller and is rich in detail and insight on a target mission.

In the evening, it was customary (almost necessary) to go to the entertainment center to look at the wall behind the bar. On this wall would be a symbol indicating our flight status for the following day. Example: a *green balloon* indicated our group was on standby, to be ready to go if we were needed. A colored balloon facing up or down was used to tell a crew if they had a mission the next day, or we used the telephone to call the sergeant. If we had a mission, we had better get to bed to be ready for the next morning.

Sure enough, the *red balloon* was facing down, so we went to our Quonset hut to try to get some sleep. About 3:00 a.m., an orderly with a flashlight came into the hut and awakened those who were scheduled to fly the mission. I dressed quickly because it was cold in the hut. I wore a heavy warm-up suit beneath my uniform to help withstand the low temperatures aloft. It was winter, and the temperatures at thirty thousand feet were fifty to seventy degrees below zero Fahrenheit.

We proceeded to the mess hall for breakfast. Most of us had bicycles to ride. If the breakfast consisted of fresh eggs (supplied by the nearby English farmers), toast, and meat sometimes, we could be certain the mission would be very difficult. After a breakfast, we met in the briefing room where we were given information relating to the forthcoming planned mission.

The meeting for briefing was conducted by a staff consisting usually of a commanding officer, an intelligence officer, a weatherman, and a spokesman to describe the details of the mission. There was a large map depicting the mission route, covered by a curtain. This curtain was not opened until the meeting was called to order. Needless to say, we all waited with bated breath to learn what our target would be. With the curtain opened and the target route displayed, there would be many groans of dismay about the difficult raid. In the briefing room, they would organize a route for us to follow. I knew someone or some ones had done an awful lot of studying to make that work. They knew where the flights were and where the gunners were, which helped us pilots tremendously.

The day was December 24, 1944 (Christmas Eve), and the target was Darmstadt, Germany. We learned the raid would be conducted by the *entire* Eighth Air Forces (a maximum effort). Our group consisted of sixty B-17 heavy bombers, and when you consider that there were seventy-two United States air bases in England, there could have been a possible two thousand heavy bombers in that raid that day. Also there were many fighter groups for our escort, to protect us from enemy fighter attacks. In addition, there were many light and medium bombers on the European continent. They would attack other German targets to divert attention away from our target.

The weather man would describe the weather conditions at the takeoff time, along the route, at the target, and our return. The intelligence man would tell us where the enemy fighters might be and how many antiaircraft guns were at the target, along the route, and at the battle lines. At the completion of the briefing, we would take a time tick (synchronizing watches) in order to take off and assemble at the proper time.

We would then go to the locker room to don our flying gear, consisting of electrically heated suits, heavy outer suits, life jackets (Mae

West), flak vests, metal helmets, two parachutes (chest and seat pack), and oxygen masks with throat microphones. While dressing, we could usually hear the German propaganda broadcasts warning us we would be shot down.

After dressing, the crew would be trucked to the flight line. The distance was several thousand yards. We would visually inspect our aircraft, including the engines and control surfaces. The four propellers were manually pulled through to distribute the oil that pooled in the bottom cylinders of the radial engines. The aircraft would have been loaded with bombs and ammunition. After boarding the aircraft, each airman (gunner, bombardier, navigator, flight engineer, pilots, and radio operator) would inspect and test their equipment. We, as pilots, had a one-hundred-item checklist to complete in order to test all the instruments and controls. Also, our fuel tanks would have been filled, holding about 2,700 gallons.

When the control tower fired a *green flare*, we would start our engines and begin our long taxi trip to the takeoff runway. Before lining up for the takeoff, we would check our engines and instruments by running them up to high revolutions per minute for manifold pressure, temperature, all instruments, gauges, and radio communication. The crew would assume their takeoff position; we would line up on the runway, put on the brakes, turn the superchargers on, put the propellers in low pitch, and run the engines to high rpm and release the brakes. The runways were about two thousand yards long, and we hoped and prayed the loaded aircraft would become airborne before we ran out of runway. When airborne, we would retract the landing gear and put on the brakes to stop the centrifugal force of the spinning wheels so that they might not interfere with the control of the aircraft.

The pilot and radio operator had communication with headquarters and other aircraft in our group. I communicated with our crew by conducting interphone checks, usually at ten-minute intervals or sooner if we encountered problems.

We would circle and climb to above fifteen thousand feet, where we would assemble with our squadron and eventually to the three-squadron group—the lead, high, and low squadrons. Normally, the group consisted of thirty-six aircraft, but today, with the maximum effort we had in excess of sixty aircraft flying. Our fuel supply would be about half gone when we assembled as a group over England and started our long, slow climb toward our target on the continent (Germany). Prior to this climb we would have put on our oxygen masks at ten thousand feet.

As we crossed the English Channel, we would be joined by our fighter escort to protect us against attacks by enemy fighter aircraft. Several times, we could see our fighter escort (usually P-51 Mustangs) engage the enemy fighter aircraft in dogfights as they attempted to attack our formation. A few enemy fighters managed to get through, and we sustained some damage from their cannons and machine guns. Our intelligence people had planned our route through flak corridors where we might be out of range from antiaircraft guns. However, there was no way we could avoid flak as we crossed the battle lines because the enemy soldiers were expert marksmen and seldom if ever missed their target if the skies were clear. We lost our squadron leader aircraft, which disintegrated from a direct hit by an exploding antiaircraft shell as we crossed over the battle lines. Our deputy squadron leader took over the lead at that point.

As we neared the target at a location that was designated as the IP (initial point), the three-squadron group would split into individual squadrons (lead, high, low) to make a forty-mile bomb run with the bomb bay doors open. (We were *low element lead in the low squadron*). The lead aircraft on the bomb run would be on automatic pilot and the bombardier, with his bomb sight, would be controlling the course of the aircraft. There was nothing the pilot and copilot could do on this bomb run except to watch instruments and report flak bursts. Each member of the crew would report flak and enemy fighter positions. When the lead bombardier dropped his bomb, the other bombardiers would drop their bombs. During this forty-mile bomb run, we were very vulnerable because we could not change course or do any evasion action that might affect the accuracy of the bombing attack. Our intelligence people had informed us that this target area was protected by four to six hundred antiaircraft guns ranging in size from 88 to 150 millimeters. They could raise a tremendous barrage of flak.

At bombs away, we would make a sharp turn, pick up airspeed as we descended, reassemble into a three-squadron group and start our long, slow descent back to our home base (Deopham Green 452nd Bomb Group). It was essential that we keep in formation for protection against enemy fighters. Any straggles that had sustained damage would be attacked by German fighters. We would report any parachutes we saw when the aircraft was abandoned. Sometimes, the only alternative when losing an engine or two would be to descend to very low altitude (on the deck to avoid enemy radar) and try to return in that manner.

As we neared our air base, each bomber would peel off from the formation, get into the landing pattern, and land at fairly close intervals with the following aircraft. If wounded were aboard the aircraft, a *red flare* would be shot, and the medics with their ambulances would pick up the wounded victims. The returning aircraft were low on fuel, and I was told that two of our aircraft were cut out of the landing pattern, couldn't make it back around, and crashed. It was a sad day.

The returning crewmen were always met by the Salvation Army personnel, served coffee and doughnuts, and greeted warmly. All in our crew were then transported to the *debriefing headquarters*, given a shot of Scotch whisky, and then interviewed. Each airman was to describe the mission as follows: How many enemy fighters seen? How many shot down? How much flak encountered? Any portable guns such as those mounted on barges or railroad cars? Was the bombing accurate? Did you have cloud cover? How many parachutes did you see? There were, no doubt, many more questions that I can't recall now.

The following day (Christmas), the song "White Christmas" was played on the public address system all day long.

Raymond says, "It was a sad day for me, and to this day, I find it hard to listen to that song. The redeeming factor was that day was stand-down (no flying) so we got to rest. We had just finished a nerve-racking day. That Christmas Eve is a day I'll always remember."

Chapter 6

Resumes Flying

On Christmas Eve 1944, Raymond Miller resumed flying after his recovery. He returned to fly with his original crew members in a brand-new B-17G, 43-38982. It was equipped with all the latest equipment, which the crew was most proud of. It was a shining one—no olive drab on it. Bombardier Harold "Hal" Kristal named the new aircraft *Warzend*.

During December, the ground troops were encountering bitter cold and snow. General Patton's Third Army was fighting its way north to Bastogne, covering a forty-mile stretch. Meanwhile, General Patch's Seventh Army was spread out over eighty-four miles of rugged terrain, holding the front of two armies assaulting Maginot fortresses west and east. Many infantry lives were lost during the Ardennes battle.

The weather had been horrible not only for the ground troops, but the weather was such that they couldn't get the airplanes off the ground. On December 24, the sky cleared so the Air Corps put forth a maximum effort with vengeance. Normally they flew around thirty-two to thirty-six bombers in a group. That mission, they flew more than sixty airplanes, anything that would get off the ground. As the first echelons were bombing the enemy, the last in the bomb stream was just warming up on the runway and ready to take off. There were two thousand heavy bombers in the air, plastering Darmstadt, Germany, and the surrounding area very hard all day long with retribution. The mission was the Battle of the Bulge in operation support of the United States ground troops in the Ardennes where the Germans made their ambitious thrust in the Ardennes in mid-December. December 24 was the largest bomber mission of the war to that date, and it was supported by nine hundred fighters.

Having lost a squadron commander and two other bombers they stayed down on the Christmas day. The December 24, 1944, mission is to be forever etched in memory for the *Warzend* crew.

On December 16, 1944, the *Stars and Stripes* paper reported that Maj. Glenn Miller's plane went missing over the English Channel, December 15, 1944. He left England in freezing rain to give a concert in Paris. His band continued to entertain the troops through the USO.

The United States Army Air Corps month after month increased their blows from the air along with those of the Royal Air Force and helped the ground forces. The intensity of assembling a thousand and more B-17s and B-24s into tactical formation, all accomplished in the span of a few hours and then getting them on their way to targets on the continent. It really was not by accident but by Eighth Air Forces Bomber Command design.

The Army Air Corps survey found that over half of the bombers that were shot down by Germans had left the protection of the main formation. The United States developed the bomb group formation to correct the problem, which evolved into the staggered combat box formation where all the B-17s could safely cover any other in their formation with their machine guns, making a formation of the bombers a dangerous target, but the use of this rigid formation meant that individual aircraft could not engage in evasive maneuvers. They had to fly constantly in a straight line, which made them vulnerable to flak. Later, German fighter aircraft used the high-speed strafing passes tactic than engaging with individual aircraft to damage them with minimum risk. The twin-engine German jet fighters had a 150 mph speed advantage and would barrel down on the formation to quickly hit and run, but their *Luftwaffe* pilots tried to avoid an aerial battle (dogfight), concentrating instead on the B-17 bombers.

B-17s rarely encounter any *Luftwaffe* jets. They were wing-heavy; the Mustang, with its laminar flow wing, could easily turn and dive with them, but in a level chase, there was no contest; the Me 262 easily sped beyond gun range. The German pilots were pretty arrogant—"arrogantly standing, inviting slaughter."

US Allied pilots never had any animosity with the pilot in the enemy aircraft. It was the only thing the airman could do, left with no choice but to fight back and defend their aircraft and crew.

The loss rate for the B-17s was 25 percent on early missions with 60 of 291 B-17s lost in combat on a second mission raid. The bombers were supported by P-47 Thunderbolt and P-38 Lightning fighter planes. But the ultimate answer, by the year 1943's end, came with the advent of long-range P-51 Mustang fighter (one of North American's best-known escort fighters of World War II) and radar aid. It resulted in the degeneration of the *Luftwaffe* as an effective interceptor force in mid-1944, and the B-17 became strategically potent. With the new Merlin engine that the Packard Company built, the Mustang was fitted with self-sealing, 108-gallon drop tank and could accompany the B-17s all the way to Berlin. The Mustang could reach a speed of four hundred mph at thirty thousand feet climbing to twenty thousand feet in five minutes and fifty-four seconds. From then on, the fighters could fly all over Germany. The escort fighters would not only fly to protect our bomber aircraft from enemy fighters but would go in ahead to the target and spray the flak gun installations, which was a great help. The B-17 pilots and crew called them *our angels*. The fighters were equipped with wing tanks that could still stand the high temperature from the exhaustion and allow them to use superchargers. The fighters kept Allied loss down and continued to erode *Luftwaffe* strength. The *Luftwaffe* was Germany's trump card in attack.

The *Luftwaffe* training organization had broken down. Inadequate pilot training and its shortsighted non-rotation of pilots made it impossible for the *Luftwaffe* to make good losses, while the Eighth Air Force expanded with completely trained American aircraft. Many flights would never have made it without the fighter planes—especially the Mustang that would pick up the bombers at the channel and escort them to their target. The B-17 proved to be inadequate for the Pacific Theater operations and was replaced with the B-24 for its range and bomb load. The B-17s—long-range, high-altitude heavy bombers—became the favorite of the European Theater.

The P-51 Mustang was a formable weapon. The Mustang at the end of the war had seen it meet with great success in all theaters of operations. Jimmy Doolittle introduced the P-51 Mustang when he began his campaign to destroy the *Luftwaffe* during his Big Week, from 20-25 February 1944. The number of Mustangs increased from then on. Mustang squadrons were sent out in formations ahead of the lead elements of the bomber formation. The Allied airpower ruled supreme, and the P-51 Mustang had done much to make it happen. While it won its fame primarily as a long-range escort fighter, it had shown excellence in every phase of operation. The Mustang fighter had shown that it could escort the bombers with impunity anywhere on assigned mission and helped air superiority over the continent. As stated, *if anything in war could be magnificent, the fighter-bomber would be it.*

The year 1944 saw development of the thirty-six-group formation where up to a thousand heavy bombers would take part in raid, planes flying in a three-dimensional formation in which boxes of aircraft with three twelve-plane squadrons were led by a target-finding, radar-equipped bomber. Aircraft were stacked one above the other to take full advantage of combined defensive firepower. The B-17s usually formed up above the cloud layer or undercast using a radio beacon system called *buncher* or *splasher*. The three-plane V shape was the basic element of all formation flying. The massive close formation did contribute to an increased incidence of midair collisions. Raymond said, "Making a left turn in formation was dangerous for the pilot in low-low element had to throttle down *real slow* and the plane flying in high element the pilot had to rev the throttle up *real fast* to keep the planes from hitting one-another."

A *splasher beacon* was a ground-based medium frequency beacon system developed by the RAF (Royal Air Force) and utilized by the USAAF (United States Army Air Force) for assembling formations. It was a somewhat complex D/F system involving several transmitters all sending the same call sign but on different frequencies. The call sign was changed very regularly to confuse the enemy. The Royal Air Force had twelve splasher sites that were made available to the Eighth Air Force in 1943. The air ministry produced a much larger number of low-power beacons known as *buncher beacons*, specifically aimed at helping the United States formations.

Raymond says, "Those beacons were all over, and when I flew by night from Texas to Tucumcari, New Mexico, it was just like driving down a highway. They were placed ten miles apart. That is where you learned instrumental training on the beam. You never got through training."

The radio aids used in formation and tracking task forces was like a GPS within. The low frequency (LF) navigation system used Morse code and the radio spectrum at 1,500 watts. The *A* and *N* Morse code letters—a dot-dash where n dash-dot —was broadcast in the opposite direction along four radials ninety degrees apart. The length and timing of the dots were entirely controlled by an operator.

The stations were set up in pairs so that a station broadcast on *A* toward the station that is sending *N*. The pilots tuned into the appropriate stations and listened on his headphones, and if on course, the two opposite Morse broadcast were merged into a steady tone. If flying *on* the beam, the tone was steady. If flying *off* the beam, the tone would drift so that either the *A* or the *N* was heard. If flying west toward *A*, which meant *N* was behind you and if you drifted left then eventually only the A Morse code and the station identifier was heard. Each station broadcast its own Morse ID every thirty seconds.

The automatic director finder (ADF) allowed a pilot to know *if* they are flying toward or away from the radio station. The method measured the signal delay between two signals or the different parts of the same and figures out which signal arrived first. If the right side of the loop antenna gets the signal first, then it is closer to the transmitter than the other side. With a fixed loop antenna, you turn the whole aircraft until both signals arrive at the same time, and then you are flying toward or away from the station. The only way to know that is having situational awareness of where you started out in relation to the station and the compass. Breaking the enemy codes gave the Allies an important advantage and saved many soldiers' lives in World War II.

For the Air Corps, minimizing losses to flak became a priority. The twenty-seven-plane box became standard for B-17s for all 1945, spread more laterally to avoid catastrophic damage to the formation from a shell burst. At the same time, wingmen flew more forward on element leaders, creating a lateral. This final variation presented flak gunners with a small target, produced excellent bomb patterns, and was both easy to fly and control. B-24s of the Second Air Division were more difficult than B-17s to fly in formation at high altitudes and with more restricted cockpit visibility, used a variation of the twenty-seven-plane box.

Initially formations were created in keeping with the prewar Air Corps doctrine that massed bombers could attack and destroy targets in daylight without fighter escort, relying on interlocking fire from their defense machine guns, almost exclusively the Browning M2 .50-caliber gun. The use of high altitude by USAAF bombers resulted in factors that demanded a tighter bomb pattern. The combat box (staggering formation) continued to be used even after the advent of fighter escort largely mitigated the threat of fighter interception. The Eighth Air Force began experimenting with different tactical formations. The practice of a concentrated formation as a *box* was the result of diagramming formation in plan, profile, and front elevation views, positioning each individual bomber in an invisible boxlike area. Heavy bombers flew in formation because that was the most effective tactic against the enemy flak and fighter defense.

Each group had its own assigned *turf* over which the group leaders would fly in a circular pattern until the exact minute they needed to join other groups in the wing or division. There was *no* waiting for straggles, which had to fend for themselves *if* late or lost. The combat was also referred to as a staggered formation. Its defense purpose was in massing the firepower of the bombers' guns, while offensively, it concentrated on a target.

Many times coming back from their target missions, they would have cloud cover underneath and a huge formation of twenty-seven to thirty-six (minus the ones lost) above and no way to get down except to peel off above and follow each other down through the cloud. Raymond said, "We were limited on fuel, trying to get back as fast as we could while being low on the approach."

In the course of Raymond's missions, he was scheduled to go back to Mannheim-Ludwigshafen, where he was wounded. He went to the briefing that morning, and when the curtain was pulled back on the map, he felt a tap on the shoulder. It was the squadron commander, who said, "Ray, you don't have to go on this mission. I know how you feel. I'll go wake up Billy Carr, and he can take your place."

Raymond was tempted to accept his offer but, on second thought, said, "Captain, I want to go on this mission. I refuse to stay home."

The captain laughed and said, "I know how you feel, but I'm offering you a chance to stand down on this mission."

Raymond, a pinnacle of inspiration and determined to see it through, says, "Obviously, I could not have anyone go in my place. I would never have forgiven myself if someone else had been injured taking my place."

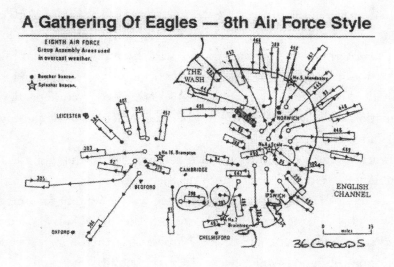

Picture of Eighth Air Forces' capability of assembling a thousand and more B-17s and 24s into thirty-six-plane formations, all accomplished in a span of a few hours, and then getting them on their way to targets on the continent. Each group had its own assigned turf over which the group leaders would fly in a circular pattern until the exact minute they needed to join other groups in the wing or division. In this layout, it represents an area about seventy-five by one hundred miles or just slightly larger than the state of New Jersey. The shaded area (down and over from The Wash) is the location of the 452nd group.

CHAPTER 7

Hanover Mission—Amid Uncertainty

The bombing mission to Hannover (English Hanover), Northwestern Germany, on the Leine River and the Midland Canal, was very heavily defended. The city was an important production center that was included in an oil campaign. It was a target for strategic bombing during World War II. A concentration camp of the Nazis was located near Hannover. The Bergen-Belsen camp was where Ann Frank died of typhus in March 1945.

As usual procedure, the pilot flew the aircraft to the target and the copilot would fly back, all the while being in formation. When they dropped the bombs on the target, they had a huge hit in the airplane and a large piece of shrapnel came through the nose of the plane. The navigator, Lt. John Nortness, had been bending over the table, looking at his map and instrument, and had just leaned back when a chunk about eight inches long and wide took off the tip of his thumb. It went on through the brake lines and cut the control cable and yoke. There was a huge hole on the cabin floor under Raymond's left foot, and he admitted, "I was afraid to look down for I didn't know what had happened."

After their bombs away, pilot 1st Lt. Harry Simmons, nodded for Raymond to take control, and then Raymond picked up the control column. It was severed and cut off, just as though it had been cut with a pair of snips, so pilot Lieutenant Simmons had to fly not only to the target but to fly back. He made a decision, with the entire crews' agreement, to land back at their home base. There was one extra-long runway in England. With no brakes, they had to devise a means to land safely. Prior to the landing, the tail turret took the parachute and hooked it to the tail wheel. The crew was put in the radio room to be all braced, and the tail gunner was told, "When we touch down, throw the parachute out the tail."

They had come in with full flaps at as slow a speed as they could without stalling, and when they touched down, the tail gunner put a parachute out the tail. As they were going down, their plan was put into place as they neared the runway. Raymond was scratching at the airspeed, and as they came down the runway, the indicator was at fifty mph. Raymond unlocked the tail wheel, and having no brakes to control the direction, he cut number one and two engines and ran up three and four and they did two ground loops off the runway into the soft grass. There was damage to the airplane undercarriage, but they all got out of the plane safely. They still have pictures of the huge chunk of flak that caused all the damage. They all were very happy to be back safely at base. Bombardier Kristal always carried Kleenex, which he used to stuff the holes to keep the cold out. It was times as this that Harold (Hal) said, "Sometimes you wondered, *What I am doing here?* There weren't any crewmen that would say they weren't scared stiff for you can't fire at flak. Flak was the scariest."

The crew had experienced some very terrifying moments. Their miracle came in the design of the aircraft, and the crewmen using all those good instructors' teachings. During a bomb run, they were particularly vulnerable since they had to stay in formation and could take no evasion action. There were bursts of flak—like popcorn popping.

Raymond said his plane flew in *low-low element*, which was very dangerous. To see an aircraft in trouble seemed like an eternity for the pilot, watching and unable to do a blessed thing to help.

If a plane was shot down, the pilot and crewmen had a survival kit that included a silk map. The map helped with location. They had been instructed to try and locate a priest for help. The pilot and crewmen were allowed to carry a side gun until 1942, and then the AAF took them. They would more likely be shot if captured with a gun rather than without it. There was a manual containing information for emergency procedures on how to face situations of being forced to make it alone while maintaining a high morale and faith in the idea they *will* eventually get back. Harold Kristal said that he still carried a gun.

There were forty-six American bomb groups in England. The sacrifices were heavy for the English people to give up all that valuable farmland for air bases. Each air base had two-thousand-yard runways, so you can imagine the thousands of acres that were given up by the British in order to accommodate all the American air bases. In return, the United States gave many sacrifices to save the British homeland from the tyrant Hitler.

After early 1943, American forces were building up in large numbers in the United Kingdom. The American air bases and our planes flew the skies along with the British to secure peace through blood, courage, and conviction with hundreds of thousands of pilots and crewmen, who *never* returned to help secure Europe from Germany.

Raymond's crew was picked as the typical American bomber crew in England. To reward them, the air force sent them to an English air base. In exchange, the English sent their typical crew to an American air base. The United States crew showed the English how to fly formation, which they didn't like. The English flew a four-engine Lancaster on night missions at a faster speed, but they didn't fly formation. They said, "We have a lot of armor plating, but we only have a tiny-winy bomb." During their exchange stay, the US crew was shown a very good time by the British.

On one occasion, Raymond was given what was called a flak leave in Scotland, where he got to visit Glasgow, Edinburgh, and many other places in Scotland for a week of R & R (rest and recreation). Raymond says, "It was beautiful country and the people were very nice. I wanted to see Cambridge University, so once, on an overnight pass, I caught the train to London. When I got into my compartment, there was an

English girl opposite me. I didn't know the railroad stations very well, so I struck up a conversation with her, told her I was going to Cambridge and asked her if she would let me know when we got to Cambridge, and much to my surprise, she got off the train with me and said, 'I'll take you to your Red Cross Officers' Club.' She walked me to the Officers' Club, and there we said good-bye, and that was my first encounter with a British lady. The next day, I went to visit Cambridge University."

Chapter 8

Thrives as Copilot

Young Second Lieutenant Raymond Miller from December 24, 1944, through March 15, 1945, resumed flying twenty more mission destinations in a B-17G *Warzend* 43-38982 after his recovery. Among his targets were the following: Darmstadt, Andernach, Kobleng, Ehrang, Fulda, Lünebach-Waxweiler, Cologne, Hamburg, Rheine, Mannheim, Freiburg-Ulm, Ansbach, Munich, Ulm, Chemnitz, Langendreer, Dortmund, Hamburg, and to Hanover on March 14, 1945. The Hanover target mission is listed in an airplane with the serial number 43-38876.

On March 15, 1945, Raymond with a crew flew to Oranienburg, Berlin, for their thirty-fifth mission to help the Russians come into Berlin to conserve it. Berlin had been the most heavily defended city in the world. It was the German Wright Field, where all their latest aircraft were tested and maintained. In a massive raid on Berlin earlier, the United States Air Corps lost sixty-nine B-17s.

Berlin would be Raymond's final mission over Germany. The crew flew in *Warzend* for this mission. Upon their mission return, the pilots were scheduled for rotation back to the United States. The crew members still had two more missions to fly. Raymond was scheduled to go home even though he had flown only twenty-two missions dropping bombs during the World War II conflict. In the interim, Raymond was assigned as duty officer in headquarters, where he kept track of the incoming phone calls relative to all the missions. Sometime after his last mission, Raymond Miller would be given rank of first lieutenant.

Raymond being in officers' barracks and the enlisted men in other barracks, all had a different approach to leisure time. The *Aero Club* was the enlisted men's main source of entertainment. Raymond said, "We had no hot water and took ice-cold showers. We had a small stove that we sometimes started with coke to get some heat. We had Plexiglas that we used to pass the time with, making ornaments, bracelets, etc. I didn't play cards. We had neighborhood pubs, sometimes close to base, that we would go to. They were family-type places where families would go in, play darts, and have discussions—no rowdiness."

On March 18, 1945, there were 1,250 American heavy bombers with a strong fighter escort who set out to attack Berlin. The entire Eighth Air Force mounted the heaviest raid of World War II against Berlin. They attacked strategic targets in and around the Third Reich's capital. On this date, it would be the *fate of the crew who inherited the* Warzend: at coordinates 52° 30' N 03° 18' E, 1458 hours, 9,000 feet altitude, heading 270 degrees, planes 43-38982 and 43-38879 collided on March 18, 1945.

Aircraft 43-38982, MACR 13559 piloted by 1st. Lt. Marvin R. Boothe of Squadron 728, hit prop wash and was swept upward under 43-38879, cutting the latter ship in half back of the bomb bay doors, where it immediately went down into the channel. Immediately after the collision, two men in 43-38982 bailed out and were seen going down, while two from the other plane were already in the water. Two aircraft, 231 and 560 from the 43-38982 groups, were ordered to remain in the distress area and patrol. One aircraft threw out ten dinghies, and when they left the distress area, they reported seeing *one* survivor in *one* of the dinghies. Air-sea rescue was contacted. Aircraft 43-38982 then proceeded on to England to crash-land at Woodridge, an RAF (Royal Air Force) base seven miles from Ipswich. Search aircraft later reported finding only empty dinghies in the area. No other word was heard from the crewmen that bailed out. On March 19, air-sea rescue reported that no one was to be found when patrols searched the area where the aircraft was to have gone down. Though search by air-sea rescue found some of the dinghies, they were empty.

The 728th Squadron diary. On March 18, 1945, one of the 452nd pilots exhibited the flying skill and tenacity of purpose that so typified the 8th Air Force. Lt. Marvin R. Boothe was flying an operational mission on that date. A plane from another element swung in and collided with his plane. By skillful and evasive action, when the pilot saw the imminence of collision, he minimized the impact to find that his plane apparently suffered little damage. However, he was forced to cut the two engines located on the wing that struck the other plane and leave the formation when parts of his plane began to fall off, a result of the collision that had not been seen at once. The nose of the plane fell off; pieces of metal continued to shower from his plane. They started dumping out any and all that they could to get more altitude. Two of his men bailed out. The bombardier and navigator had been hurt, so Lieutenant Boothe decided to try to get the plane and his crew back to his base by skillful flying. He restarted one engine as they approached the cliffs of Dover to get more altitude. Although his plane was actually disintegrating in midair, Lieutenant Boothe brought his plane back to a Royal Air Force base at Woodbridge, England. The plane was in such a condition that it was salvaged, but the injured men had been brought safely to medical aid. Lieutenant Boothe, in the modest manner of all exceptional pilots, thought it was no more than a *rough one.*

Aircraft 43-38982: 2nd Lt. George A. Knoerl, navigator, and waist gunner S/Sgt. James C. Kennemer—both on their sixteenth mission—bailed out into the channel, listed as POW/MIA. Seven of the crewmen returned.

Raymond became acquainted with the new crew that inherited *Warzend,* and they advised him that the Germans had become desperate, sending up very inexperienced pilots who tried to ram the B-17s. Many times, it wasn't successful and they only succeeded in making fatal plunges into the ground after trying to crash into the aircraft. They stated that "*Warzend* survived and continued to fly until the end of the war in Europe and that the aircraft had been ferried back to the United States." The 728th Squadron diary stated that *Warzend* was in such a condition that it was salvaged. Raymond says, "As far as I know, it may be stored back in the desert out west in Arizona or New Mexico." With no concrete record, *Warzend*'s fate remains a mystery.

Victory in Europe (VE) *Day* was when Germany surrendered unconditionally to the Allies on May 8, 1945. The United States Air Force B-17 bombers, the Flying Fortresses, led the onslaught that devastated the Germans. In addition to strategic missions, the air supported the ground troop's forces and carried out interdictory operations and helped prepare for the invasion of Normandy by hitting airfields, bridges, V-weapon sites, and other objects, and struck coastal defenses on D-Day, 6 June 1944. In preparation for Operation Overload, General Omar Bradley used the air force as forward artillery for the ground troops in support of the breakthrough task at Saint-Lô. With forces on the ground, the distance was measured not in miles but in yards.

Shortly after D-Day, Lt. Gen. Lesley J. McNair was killed during Operation Cobra, which was part of the Battle of Normandy. The United Stated Army's Eighth Air Force started carpet bombing near Saint-Lô, France. The Army Air Corps accidently came in over Allied troops with high explosives and fragmentation bombs. The bomber pilots' visibility was impaired by bad weather—a malfunction where the lead ship would drop early. McNair was observing the Thirtieth Infantry Division's preparations for deployment to Saint-Lô. As frequently as he could, he would visit the front lines. A bomb landed squarely on McNair in a foxhole. More than 130 American soldiers were killed and 621 soldiers were wounded. It was a tragic accident. War is not pretty but ugly.

Lieutenant General McNair, commanding chief of the Army Ground Forces, had received a Purple Heart when wounded in the North African Campaign. Lt. Gen. Lesley McNair was one of the highest-ranking American officers killed in World War II. McNair's son, Col. Douglas McNair was killed two weeks later by a sniper in Guam. Hoosier Ernie Pyle, famed war correspondent, survived the bombing. He said it was "the most sustained horrible thing I've ever gone through."

Air cooperation with the ground forces became closer than ever. The generals on the ground relied heavily on tactical air force to reconnoiter and give them ample warning of any serious danger from the source. Each day the army order was issued to all elements, including the air, specifying "the color of the day"—that is, which color was to be displayed on all vehicles that day—so that all ground vehicles could be spotted. As a result of this, the air force found the panels were an excellent identification, which eliminated most of their earlier worries about bombing Allied columns.

The B-17 Flying Fortresses flew the sky slowly but surely, knocking the German *Luftwaffe* strength out of the skies and smashing vital targets of Germany round the clock. The air offensive reduced the Nazi capacity to wage war on the ground. The Germans were known for using church belfries as observation posts. They were ruthless about hiding behind civilians in occupied territory as at Saint-Lô.

The brave American airmen who flew the dangerous mission across the English Channel against insurmountable odds were heroes risking their lives in the pursuit of freedom. Mission-ready, pilots were permutation professionals; they depended on one another's objectivity. By early 1944, the average fighter pilot entering combat had logged at least 450 hours, usually including 250 hours in training. In mid-1944, the Army Air Forces had 2.6 million people and nearly eighty thousand aircraft of all types.

Normal flight missions were six to nine hours. The weather proved to be the greatest problem to the heavy bombers during a bombing raid—worse than the mission. No cloud cover meant that bombers were easy prey for Nazi fighters and antiaircraft guns. B-17s flying in formation were overloaded vapor trails traced the weaving path of their fighter escorts. "Strong wind used fuel," bombardier Harold Kristal said. "We came in on fumes. Some missions we had to divert (sock-in) and fly to another airport. Some missions we would sweat it out."

The flight training of a pilot was a top priority for the Army Air Force and the principal object of Air Corps training. The success and safety of the crew relied on the pilot, who was the air commander. Raymond learned firsthand the importance of the pilot and his crew's knowledge when they sacrificed to save his life.

Raymond says much could never have been done without the tremendous amount of resources, arms, ammunition, and fuel that was brought across the Atlantic by the merchant marines who were exposed to all those dangers and casualties. They were some of the real heroes. A lot of them were killed when their ships went down.

There was a fraternization violation policy of the uniform code and military justice. While in Norwich, England, one day, Raymond recalls an incident involving some American servicemen being questioned by the British military police (MP). It was an army policy for officers and non-officers not to fraternize off duty, but on this one particular occasion, Lieutenant Miller and his radio operator were goofing around, resulting with George Culnon wearing Raymond's jacket with white stripes, a clear indication of the rank of an officer. The MP saluted George, whom he thought was an officer. Raymond said that "it left the men laughing for some time after."

While standing around, they saw some Englishmen driving their livestock right through the middle of town. The landscape, farms, and garden plots were so different than in America. They had what you call the *allotment act* of small plots.

In England, there were those buzz bombs that would bring about terror for the people. Germany had developed flying bombs that were launched over England. The Argus 109-104's pulse engine range was 150 miles, with a maximum speed of 393 mph. The 1,870-lb amatol warhead was like a small airplane. The weapons were launched from ground sites through the use of ramps fitted with steam or chemical catapults. Sites the Germans used to launch them were constructed in the Northern French region. They used slave labor at a notorious underground plant to build some of the bombs near Nordhausen. Raymond said that you never knew where they would land. Once, one exploded and lifted his feet up off the ground, which was the best way to describe the sensation that was felt. It was fortunate that it wasn't close. People learned in a short time that at the end of a *V-1's buzz* was a warning to get to a shelter for it was headed for the ground. They only struck their targets 25 percent of the time. These buzz bomb weapons had little impact on the war, but they killed 6,184 innocent people, and they injured 17, 981 people. From the odd sound of the V-1's engine, the British dubbed them *buzz bombs* and *doodlebugs*.

On missions, Raymond said as they were climbing, they could see rocket trails. To combat the buzz bombs' threat, antiaircraft guns were deployed for defense. They were soon joined by the United States fighter airplanes, improvements were made in aerial interception and from the ground new tools aided the fight. Finally, the threat ended when Allied troops overran the German launch positions in France and the Low Countries. The V-1 buzz bombs were no longer able to hit targets in Britain.

On one mission, Raymond's crew was sent to Western England to Wales and the weather turned bad. They had on all their heavy equipment, with no clothing to walk around in during the time they were grounded (weathered-in) over there. Before the activity they had to do, Raymond wore a blister on his foot that got infected. When they got back to the base, he was put in the infirmary and their mission put on stand-down. The crew was scheduled to fly the next day. The replacement crew that took their place on the mission was shot down by a *Luftwaffe* fighter plane. The B-17 plane and the whole crew were lost.

There was a target mission to Munich on February 25, 1945. The Alps setting, Raymond felt, was at the right timing as their target was Munich. The Alps are just eighty kilometers south of Munich, the cradle of the Nazi beast. Eagle's Nest, Hitler's house was in the Alps. Eagle's Nest is located on a sharp peak overlooking Berchtesgaden. The Alpine mountains are some of the most tranquil and beautiful landscapes, like a picture. Raymond said, "There was a sense of calming and soothing. The Alps could be seen for two hundred miles from the air."

1st Lt. Raymond Miller Pilot

Many American airmen thought they would not make it home for they knew the odds were high against them. Without discipline and teamwork, they'd all be killed. Flying combat was deadly serious. The slight lapse of judgment would cause an explosive collision and death for the crew. German flak and small-arms fire were intense. Yet for the pilots, the sky became their domain.

Chapter 9

Flying Fortress

With the attack on Pearl Harbor, the United States Army Air Force started deploying their B-17s to England. England's Royal Air Force lacked a true heavy bomber at the start of World War II. In August of 1942, American B-17s flew their first raid over occupied Europe.

The Boeing B-17 Flying Fortress is a four-engine heavy bomber aircraft developed for the United States Army Air Corps. The first design began on 18 June 1934, and the prototype made a successful flight at Boeing Field on July 1935. The B-17 heavy bomber would fly in close formation, bristled with machine guns, and battled antiaircraft fire and swarms of German fighters to reach their targets. The B-17 was primarily employed by the USAAF in the strategic bombing campaign of World War II. The aircraft was a potent, high-flying long-range bomber that was able to defend itself and returned home despite being an ex-weapon system, dropping more bombs than any other United States aircraft in World War II.

The B-17 Flying Fortress, the United States' heavy bomber, was operational all through the war. With smaller numbers of B-24 Liberators, the Fortress spearheaded the USAAF's *daylight offensive* bombing operations against Europe and the RAF (Royal Air Force) who had the *nighttime offense* bombing, providing round-the-clock attacks that penetrated deep into enemy territory against German industrial and military targets.

Raymond copiloted B-17 aircraft and commanded crews in aerial offensives against the enemy, which required him to have a thorough knowledge of operation and maintenance of the B-17 aircraft, as well as radio navigation, radio aids, first aid, meteorology, instrument flying, local flying rules, and CCA rules and regulations. The checklist that the pilot and copilot would go through together before takeoff was a measure to prevent accidents on the plane.

Harry Simmons and Raymond flew a B-17F Flying Fortress across the ocean that had no chin. It flew at only 180 mph. Later overseas, they were introduced to the new B-17G with a chin. The United States Air Force made many changes with the B-17s flying in close formation. To reach their target, B-17s hoisting load of bombs into the sky battled through storms of antiaircraft fire and swarms of German fighters.

The pilots' seats were the most comfortable place on the plane, with a very good view. Preparing to fly out on a target mission, pilots would take off at thirty-second intervals with a group of aircraft, which would take approximately thirty minutes to get them airborne. Each plane had to takeoff at the precise second in order to maintain required flight separation. Sometimes takeoffs were visual, and pilots would have several hundred feet of altitude before enlisting in squadron assembly and go on instrument. Both pilots making corrections required complete cooperation. There were times when they made instrument takeoffs with the pilot totally on instrument while the copilot was observing the conditions of the runway. For the pilots, it was a harrowing experience knowing they were responsible for the crew's safety. There were missions where there used to be a few corridors; they would be closed up. Flak at times was light and inaccurate over target, and other times, there were plenty of prayers said.

Upon reaching 200 feet of altitude, takeoff power was reduced to climb power, and the pilot would immediately start a left turn with 15 degrees of bank throughout the climb out. Meanwhile, the airplane was held constant at 150 mph, the rate of climb was at 200 feet per minute. On their radio direction finder, the pilot tuned to *base radio beacon* frequency with the needle kept on 270 degrees, which indicated that the field and beacon were always off to the left wing tip. Between the 270 degrees and the 15 degrees of bank, this position in relation to the field was held constant while spiraling counterclockwise to altitude. With the flight pattern being corkscrew, the base was being represented by the point on the screw. At times, a position was held until they broke out of the clouds from a few thousand feet to over 15,000 feet. They went up the spiral corkscrew turn at thirty-second intervals and within 10 miles in either direction in clouds and total darkness with no margin for error. There were collisions in the overcast. The lead ship flying in a circle above fired assigned-color magnesium flares to identify his aircraft so they could form on him.

B-17s flew at altitude exceeding twenty thousand feet, and in such cold temperatures, left a visible trail of condensed water vapor, and ice crystals would form from the exhaust stacks, which made what was known as contrails. This made them easy prey for the German jet pilots.

When there were one hundred aircrafts, they circled in the air and joined other groups. It was all mapped out to accomplish that many aircraft to fly over an area about the size of New Jersey to get that aircraft into the air at one time. They had two-thousand-yard runways that they were fortunate at having to get off on at thirty-second intervals. They went down through the clouds by instrument, holding their airspeed while descending constantly and looking for prop wash before and behind them. Raymond says, "Sometimes we were just lucky to get through. Sometimes we'd break out of the undercast maybe two or three hundred feet above the ground level. At our altitude, if we didn't have cloud cover beneath and we could break out, we could see for two hundred miles."

When they had to cross the battle line coming and going, Raymond says, "I have to admit we prayed for a cloud cover because if you went across, they'd shoot those 88s at you, and they could get the leader. So we prayed, as we went across, to have a cloud cover to get to the line."

Flight missions' crews never knew what may come next. There were missions when they had colossal tailwinds. A one-hundred-mile-an-hour jet stream behind them, usually from west to east, and the ground speed would be tremendous going to a target, but when they had to rally and come back, they had to fight headwinds. The Germans may be waiting with railroad or barge guns, and they threw up everything they had. It wasn't known where they were. The ground speed was way less, and they had to battle and hope on their way past the flak that they encountered. During a bomb run, they were particularly vulnerable since they had to stay in formation and could take no evasion action. Once through the final run, they'd gather up and head for home.

The light and medium bombers would attack to divert the German fighters away from the B-17s. To some extent, the B-17s weren't exposed to great groups of fighters. The US P-51s would escort them, and they did a great deal of dogfighting to keep those German fighters away from the B-17s. Some chaff ships flew in a tremendous altitude, maybe thirty-five thousand feet over the target, and opened their bomb bay door and dropped as much chaff as they could on the German continent.

Splasher beacons were ground-based medium frequency beacon systems developed by the RAF (Royal Air Force) and utilized by the USAAF for assembling formation. It was a somewhat complex D/F system involving several transmitters all sending the same call sign, but on different frequencies. The call sign was changed very regularly to confuse the enemy. The RAF had twelve *splasher* sites that were made available to the Eighth Air Force in 1943. The air ministry produced a much larger number of low-power beacons known as *buncher beacons*, specifically aimed at helping the United States formations.

The highest losses for the B-17 Flying Fortress bomber occurred from February 1944 through May 1944, which was the group's first four months of combat. Each month, there would be a steady increase in the loss of the heavy bombers—with May being the heaviest with 237 B-17s lost by the Eighth Air Forces. During those four months, over 500 airmen from the Eighth Air Forces would give their lives for their country, while 8,500 others would be taken prisoners. Some 452nd men flew damaged B-17s to neutral countries. Total losses from the Eighth Air Force are nearly 3,200 B-17s lost outright in combat action and another 2,500 so badly damaged that they were no longer operational. Of the flying squadron that started out with the 452nd, only the 729th remains with the 452nd, flying C-17s as an airlift squadron.

Germany captured approximately forty B-17s that crash-landed or were forced down. These were refurbished, with a dozen put back into the air, given German national markings, and were used to determine the B-17s vulnerabilities and to train German interceptor pilots in attack tactics. Some were used for other purposes as well, and some, with their Allied markings, were used by the *Luftwaffe* in attempts to infiltrate B-17 bombing formations and report on their positions and altitudes. The practice was initially successful, but Army Air Force combat aircrews quickly developed and established standard procedures to first warn off and then fire upon any *stranger* trying to join a group's formation. There was a light-blinking code for recognition of friendly aircraft. The Japanese captured at least three and restored them to flying condition. Japan had them flown to Japan, where they were used to evaluate the design and to develop tactics to be used against B-17s.

The United States Army's Eighth Air Forces B-17 Bomber, the Flying Fortresses, led the onslaught that devastated Germany with relentless bombing, which paid off and contributed to the German surrender. The Boeing B-17 Flying Fortress heavy bombers went through numerous upgrades, with a catalogue of the variants and specific unique elements of each variant and/or design changes to improve the effectiveness, range, and load capacity. The obvious change was a redesigned vertical stabilizer. The first production models of the B-17, B-17A, and B-17B entered the service in 1939 and were the fastest as well as the highest-flying bombers in the world. They were the first aircraft in the world to enter service with turbocharged engines. The B-17C changed, using more powerful engine, more machine guns, more armor, and self-sealing fuel tanks.

B-17D had minor changes, with different engine cowling flaps and an extra pair of machine guns. B-17E was the first model primarily focused on offensive warfare. The most visible change was the addition of a vertical tail fin forward of the now-larger tail. This feature increased flight stability, especially during high-altitude bomb runs. The addition of a pair of .50-caliber machine guns in a tail turret required a completely redesigned rear fuselage, resulting in a foot longer aircraft. The third big change was the installation of powered turrets in the ventral and tail fin positions. The add-ons made for a somewhat slower but eminently more defensible aircraft. On July 1, 1942, the first B-17E arrived in Britain. Six weeks later, eighteen Flying Fortresses launched their first raid against Nazi Europe, hitting rail yards and adjacent buildings as primary targets. In the winter of 1942-43, the air war in Northwest Europe accelerated.

B-17Fs were the primary versions flying for the Eighth Air Forces in 1943, and had standardized the manned Sperry ball turret for ventral defense, along with an enlarged, nearly frameless Plexiglas bombardier's nose enclosed for much improved forward vision along with increased capacity and extended range and combat radius. The F series was found to be tail-heavy once in combat and proved almost immediately to have inadequate defensive protection when attacked from the front. The weight of gunners and ammunition when combat-loaded moved the center of gravity rearward from its design point and forced constant use of the elevator trim tab, stressing that component. It was the first B-17 variant to be produced at the same time by Boeing, Lockheed/Vega, and Douglas. From the outside, the F model closely resembled the E model; only the unframed, bubble-style Plexiglas nose appeared different. The (over) four hundred changes to the B-17F made a better bomber with the new Wright R-1820-97 Cyclone engines, paddle-bladed propellers, a stronger undercarriage, external bomb racks, better brakes, carburetor intake filters, etc.

Under license of the United States government during World War II, the Wright Cyclone nine-cylinder radial engines were built by the Studebaker Corporation based out of South Bend, Indiana.

Raymond flew a B-17F that had no chin across the ocean. It flew at only 180 mph. Later they were introduced to the new B-17G with a chin. The Boeing B-17G *Champaign Girl* was one of the first metal-finished airplanes to roll off the assembly line. In late 1943, the air forces discarded the camouflage paint. Paint on airplanes added another five hundred pounds and slowed the plane down. Combat crews were initially concerned of being singled out by the *Luftwaffe* fighters, but there were no significant loss increase from the change.

The B-17Fs participated in the January 27, 1943, raid on the submarine facilities at Wilhelmshaven, the first United States Army Air Forces mission over Germany. The *Luftwaffe* pilots quickly identified the B-17's vulnerability to head-on attacks.

The B-17Gs were the most numerous, with improved turbochargers on their four 1,200-hp Wright Cyclone engines that enabled them to cruise at up to 3,500 feet, and their maximum load was 9,600 pounds. The maximum speed of this version was 287 mph, and the gas load was 2,810 gallons of one-hundred-octane gas. The B-17G was introduced onto the Fortress production line in mid-1943, with the most readily noticeable design to eliminate a weakness in head-on attacks by adding the power-operated *Bendix* turret, a chin-type turret sticking out below the nose. The afterthought turret was equipped with two Browning .50 caliber machine guns that addressed the B-17's vulnerability. The waist guns were permanently enclosed behind windows instead of being mounted behind removable hatches. This made the rear fuselage somewhat less drafty and gave protection for the waist gunner area that had been left wide open. The cheek nose guns introduced on the late B-17F were retained but were staggered so that the left gun was in the forward side window and the right gun was in the middle side window, which reversed the positions used on the "F" series. The cheek gun mounts bulged somewhat outward into the air stream, which helped to improve the forward view from the cheek gun positions.

The G model sported the defensive firepower of thirteen Browning .50 caliber machine guns in the new chin turret that included two chin guns, two cheek guns, two dorsal turret guns, two ventral turret guns, two waist guns, tail guns, and one gun in the roof of the radio operator's position. The *Cheyenne* tail gun modifications were incorporated with mountings that had a reflector gunsight instead of the previous ring and bead. The B-17Gs were five inches shorter than the earlier versions. In later versions, the waist gun position was staggered so that the two gunners would not get in each other's way. The radio compartment gun was not installed, and the ammunition capacity of the waist guns was increased to six hundred rounds per gun. The designs of the gun stations were finalized, and other adjustments were completed.

There was an IFF device (meaning identification, friend or foe), which was, at that time, a very secret device so if they were to go down, they were to blow it up. Instead of a ball turret, which most of bombers had, the lead plane had a ball under there that contained a radar device. It became apparent to the enemy that a plane with the device was the aircraft that they would attempt to shoot down. Until IFF became available, blips could not be identified.

The formidable B-17 design went through eight major changes over the course of its production, culminating in the B-17G, differing from its immediate processor by the addition of a chin turret. It was the final version of the Flying Fortress.

In the European Theater of Operations, the Eighth Air Force and Fifteenth Air Force were the two United States Army Air Forces that bore the burden of the fighting. The B-17 Fortress and the B-24 Liberator were used by the United States Air Forces as long-range, high-altitude, four-engine heavy bombers. The B-24 had a superior speed, range, and bomb loads to the B-17. The B-17 could hold formation in high altitudes while the B-24 could not maintain formation in altitudes above twenty-one thousand feet, making it more vulnerable to antiaircraft artillery and fighter attack. The B-17 Flying Fortress bomber was the United States's workhorse during World War II.

Raymond Miller really enjoyed flying the B-17G and said, "Its graceful lines and its ability to fly at higher altitudes and most of all its ruggedness. The survival rate for ditching was far more likely to stay intact. The B-17 was like a *mother hen*. She took us under her wings for protection. She did her very best to keep us out of harm's way. She wanted to keep flying under all conditions, including adverse weather, despite enemy actions resulting in severe damage, and had the ability to absorb the damage in order to bring the crew home safely.

"They B-17 carried fewer bombs and couldn't fly as far as the B-24. It was like a *faithful dog* who always forgave us for the mistakes we made. She was always willing to protect us by exerting her tremendous firepower and her ability to answer our controls. She carried tremendous loads of fuel, bombs, and ammunition to help us succeed in our mission to thwart the enemies' intention to take our freedom. The crew members felt the heavy B-17 features saved their lives and that it wouldn't let them down on a mission and returned them to their home base. Many times, pilots touched down with the B-17 riddled with flak holes and smoking with engines out. It was an airplane that seemed to want to fly. When I view the beautiful B-17, it reminds me of memories that have remained with me for nearly seventy years."

As World War II intensified, the bombers needed additional armaments and armor, and each B-17 series to follow was more heavily armed. The aircraft served in every World War II combat zone. For the Army Air Forces, the Flying Fortress lived up to its given trademark name. The design was a miracle whether a crew made it back or not. Many B-17Gs were converted for other missions such as cargo hauling, engine testing, reconnaissance, and search and rescue duties.

At Deopham Green crews would fly the B-17 aircraft to Ireland to get a load of Irish whiskey to have at the base. The air forces used pure Scotch whiskey for battle-savvy crewmen upon their return from a mission.

The B-17 established itself as an effective weapons system, dropping more bombs than any other aircraft in World War II. Of the 1.5 million metric tons of bombs dropped on Germany and its occupied territories, 640,000 tons were dropped from United States B-17 aircraft. Thirty-two B-17-equipped overseas combat groups' inventories peaked in August 1944 at 4,574 USAAF aircraft worldwide.

B-17 Flying Fortress squadrons from Deopham Green airfield lost 450 men and 158 aircraft from February 1944 through April 1945, when they went on the last of the 250 missions even at the latter part of the war, because of the massive formation taking off in England's legendary fog and a barrage of flak they encountered over their targets. The Eighth Air Forces had twenty-eight thousand killed and twenty-nine thousand POWs.

There were 8,680 B-17s produced between July 1943 and April 1945. The G was the most numerous B-17 variant: 4,035 B-17Gs by Boeing, 2,395 by Douglas, and 2,250 by Lockheed/Vega. The vast majority of surviving B-17s is the G design.

Army Air Forces aircraft statistics. There were 1,693,565 missions flown by combat aircraft. Fifty-five percent of these 32,263 aircraft were lost in action.

Chapter 10

Bomb Load

The B-17's usual bomb load was about two-and-half tons. It had two racks—each rack held four five-hundred-pound GP *(general-purpose) bombs* while on top of each was a 550-pound cluster of *thermite bombs* of six pounds each. These were incendiary bombs. Each bomb had fins at the tail and a streamlining plate at the front. Also each bomb had two fuses (one front and one back) and propellers would spin off to arm the bomb. The *cluster bombs* had their incendiaries timed so that after the propellers spun off, the timing mechanism would explode these cluster bombs about five-hundred feet above the ground and scatter the six-pound bombs. Every sixth six-pound incendiary had an explosive charge so the enemy fire fighters didn't know which incendiary would explode. In World War II, the Nazi Regime began the campaign with the use of incendiary bombings with the bombing of Warsaw and then, London Blitz, Moscow, and other sites. Incendiary bombs have been used since ancient times. Their use in combat proved to be a highly effective weapon, destroying armored vehicles, tanks, and spraying a battlefield. They didn't just destroy small things, but the civilian destruction caused by such weapons quickly earned them a reputation as *terror weapon*.

The *five-hundred general purpose bombs* exploded on contact but could be fused to penetrate before exploding. After the airplane was safely in flight, the bombardier could manually pull all the safety pins in the bomb, then they would be armed. That usually meant they were to drop the bombs.

On one of Raymond's flying missions, the bombs did not part the aircraft, but were jammed in the bomb bay. The bomb load that day was rather unusual in that instead of having the bombs hung directly to the bomb shackles, it was decided they could increase the load by utilizing cables and having two bombs shackled to each shackle. This resulted in the bombs being unable to release cleanly because the downward force was transmitted at an angle that was unsuitable for operation of the shackles, resulting in the bombs being what they called hung (in other words, they didn't let go). They had three or four layers on each side of the bomb bay with the situation where the lower ones that would exit the aircraft first were stuck at the bottom and all the bombs had released and were lying on top of them. That wasn't so bad, except for the fact that the movement was enough to have pulled out arming wires. With the fusing mechanism, there is a fuse on the nose and tail of each bomb, and these propellers were spinning free, and when they spun off, the bombs would be live. To make matters worse, on the top of each of these roll bombs were bombs on top of the others. The top ones were *550-pound, aimable cluster incendiary bombs*, one on each side of the bomb bay—those operated differently from the others. The *general purpose bombs* were detonated by impact with whatever target that they may be landing on. The *incendiary bombs* were operated in the air before striking the target and then spread out over a very large area and creating multiple fires. There may be fifty to a hundred individual bombs in one *550-pound incendiary bomb*, and they had it in on each side of the bomb bay, on top on all the other *general purpose bombs*.

When *bombardier* 2nd Lt. Harold Kristal got back to the bomb bay, he had no time to lose because once those propellers spun off those top bombs. It was a time mechanism so the bomb is going to think it was about five hundred to one thousand feet above the ground. It was going to be an internal explosion and blow all these smaller bombs all over the place. Of course, the smaller bombs were *incendiary bombs,* and it wouldn't take very long before they would have a big fire that would have destroyed the aircraft in a very short period of time. Harold knew it was his job to figure out how to get rid of them dang *things* quickly.

The clothing worn to fly a mission was a lot for it was very cold—normally minus fifty degrees centigrade below zero. Wearing a lot of clothing made a very thick package. Air crewmen wore a flak suit and *Mae West* life vest, and over it all, they wore a parachute harness. The harness they wore accommodated a chest pack that actually would be just over the lower chest and probably stick out maybe eight to ten inches. Because of that, Harold was unable to go out there on this catwalk with the bomb bay doors wide open without a parachute. Harold wearing so much outer clothing made him very susceptible to being caught by a bomb fin *if* the bombs decided to drop, and he would have gone right out with them. Harold knew he had to get rid of *them things* in a hurry, so he took his chances. He had one riser from the harness and handed it to the radio operator, George Culnon, saying, "Hang onto this thing for dear life because my dear life is in your hands. If I am pulled out of the airplane, the only way that I am going to keep from falling all the way to the ground is your holding onto that riser from that harness. At which time, I will proceed to probe around to see what I can do to loosen the bombs."

The bombs had to be loosened from the bottom and had several thousand pounds resting on them. They were all jammed in there, so Harold started fiddling around. They were twenty-five thousand feet above the ground. At that point, in addition to all the clothing he was wearing, he had to also carry a walk-around oxygen bottle because at that altitude, they needed oxygen. Harold proceeded to fiddle around with the release mechanism, which was called a *shackle,* and it finally decided it would let go of the whole stack at once on one side, one right after the other. Fortunately, he was clear. Out it went, and it was before the incendiary at the top exploded, so he decided to go to the other side and do the same. After a little while, the same thing happened. They all fell out at the same time including the top bomb, which was the *cluster incendiary bomb.* He was basically finished at that time. He asked the radio operator to call the pilot to have him close the bomb bay doors. Once they were closed, the radio operator handed him the riser that he was holding onto. Harold proceeded back to his position at the nose of the airplane to regain some equanimity.

On the onset, the bombardier was really pressed for time for the propellers had been spinning when he got to them. They were where Harold was (catwalk), six or seven inches wide. Made out of metal, they ran the length of the bomb bay, and then there were the racks of bombs on each side—one set on left, one set on right.

On the way back from the target, a bomb tumbled off an airplane above their plane in the formation and just missed them. Harold had looked up and saw that it had fallen on the right-hand bomb bay door and damaged it and forced it open enough to roll out, which was why it was tumbling. The pilots had to land with those bombs lying on the doors. "No bomb had gone off," Harold said. "That was just luck!"

The Army Air Forces never tried to attach more cable to increase the line again. The shackles were never designed to have force applied at an angle. It was meant for the force to be downward.

Harold would devise a device to help dislodge the bombs with. He wanted to be able to manipulate the shackles at a distance so that his clothing would not get caught on the fins. It was a very simple device that he called his Bomb Kicker Outer. It was made with a piece of lightweight steel with a small Y welded on the end of it.

A bombardier sits right in the Plexiglas nose of a Fort, so he sees everything that the eye can see of what is laid out in front of him. On a mission once, the aircraft was nearing a target location, and the three squadrons split into individual squadrons to make a forty-mile bomb run. Copilot Raymond Miller's plane would be in low-element lead. From high altitude, Harold Kristal used the Norden bombsight, known as the Blue Ox. The United States Army accrued it in 1944 from the navy, having previously used the Sperry. The device would determine, from variable input by the bombardier, the point at which the aircraft bombs should be released to hit the target.

The Norden bombsight consisted of two main parts, a stabilizer and a sight-head. The stabilizer was a platform that was kept level by a series of gyroscopes and was attached to the plane's autopilot, which would fly the plane to the precise location. The sight was a mechanical analog computer made up of motors, gears, gyros, mirrors, levers, and a telescope, which allowed the bomber's deadly payload to be dropped at exactly the right moment needed to hit the target.

The bombardier programmed the mechanical analog computer with the airspeed, wind speed and direction, altitude, and angle of drift. With this information, the bombsight would calculate the trajectory of the bomb. Upon the plane approaching the target, the pilot would be turned to autopilot, which would fly the plane to the precise location and release the bomb over the target. There was nothing for the pilots to do during the bomb run except watch instruments and report flak. Until the bombardier cleared for "bombs away" for the pilots, the bombardier was in complete control—mastery of the plane. The bombardier was well trained for his duty. Second Lieutenant Kristal had finished a nerve-racking target mission. He could take pride in the knowledge that his exuberant morale and display of courage had prevented his crew from being blown out of the sky.

If for some reason a mission had to be aborted, a code message would be transmitted to the radio operator and pilot that the mission had been scrubbed. There were times the bomb load was taken back to base, which wasn't preferred. Pilots dropped them in the English Channel or on what was called a target of opportunity. Targets of opportunity meant legitimate military targets that should have a clear mandate but often weren't the case.

The Norden bombsight that Harold used was so secret that he had to take a *Bombardier's Code of Honor* to swear *as guardian* to keep the secrecy of all confidential information on the American bombsight. Because of the importance and sensitive nature of the technology, its sight was a very closely guarded secret and stored in a fortified building area when not in use.

Carl Norden, a Dutch engineer who came to the United States in 1904, designed the bombsight for the United States Navy. Norden was raised in Java and educated in Switzerland. He worked with Elmer Sperry on gyrostabilizers until 1913. He began designing the bombsight for the United States Navy in 1920. Elmer Perry designed the Perry bombsight for the army, but the army found the Norden bombsight to be a far better design. The daylight strategy became a viable option to take the war over to Germany and bring the war to a quick end. The Norden bombsight was used on the B-29 *Enola Gay* to drop the atomic bomb on Hiroshima on August 6, 1945. The B-29 was the most powerful, most destructive weapon of World War II. After the war, and the high-tech equipment era of the jet, the Norden bombsight was no longer used and became obsolete. Only one person was needed to operate the jet-era equipment.

Toward the end of 1944 and in 1945, when the Air Corps was short on bombardiers, a togglier did the same job as the bombardier except he did not use the Norden bombsight to calculate where to release the bombs. The tactic change was felt to be more accurate in having one bombardier open the bomb bay doors from the lead aircraft; the togglier opened the doors on his aircraft. When the lead bombardier dropped his bombs, all the other bombardiers or toggliers in the formation dropped at same time—it fell on the lead bombardier to accurately hit the target. The togglier's job during a bomb run was to sit in the nose of the aircraft and watch the lead bomber. The togglier job was assigned the task of flipping a switch to drop the bombs. The togglier was an enlisted man doing a job similar to a bombardier but less complicated. Before and after the actual bomb run, he would resume his usual position on the aircraft, which was that of gunner. Five percent in the formation had toggliers.

Various visual systems were used to designate the lead bomber other than position since that designation could, due to circumstance, change during the course of an attack. Systems such as the firing of specifically colored flares were used as visual aids for the other bombers within the formation.

To pin that enlisted bombardiers and toggliers were the same is not accurate since the bombardiers had very intense two to three months of training to earn their bombardier wings—a special insignia common to both enlisted and commissioned bombardiers. On the aircraft that Raymond flew, Harold served as bombardier other than for a very few times at the end of the war, when toggliers were used. Descriptions of visual aids during a typical bomb run over the course of the war from different time periods were inconsistent since war tends to be a learn-as-you-go experience.

On target missions, they had in their plane what was called window chaff, packages of small aluminum strips—like glittering tinsel used to decorate Christmas trees. The radio operator during a bomb run would have a chance to throw this chaff down through a chute. It was dropped by formations to scramble German radar and make it difficult to pick up on the raiders' real position. The air force thought that it would interfere with the radar the enemy used to guide their guns. Harold Kristal stated that after the war, that tinsel could be seen all over, and the people who visited Germany wondered what it was for.

Chapter 11

USAF Postwar Adoption

When the European war was over, the airmen could relax a bit. Some came home, some stayed in the Army Air Corps or the reserves. Most understood that the war was over, but for some, to rehabilitate after combat wasn't as easy, and they never found any peace within. So many lives were lost unnecessarily. The *Luftwaffe* fought to its last drop of fuel—if not to its last aircraft or pilot. At the finish, Germany's aircraft sat with their fuel tanks empty.

At the same time, Lieutenant General Patch, European ground commander of the Seventh Army, was summoned to Washington DC on a matter of urgency. Patch wanted to be sent back to the Pacific, but those hopes were shattered when he received the war department orders for a six-week duty. Chief of Staff Gen. George C. Marshall wanted to examine into reorganization of the War Department for postwar adoptions and tapped General Patch to head what came to be called The Patch Board.

Lt. Gen. Alexander "Sandy" Patch, a graduate of West Point, was an infantryman in both World War I and World War II. He had a modest and unassuming manner and quietly went about doing his job. He played a low profile and never cared for the spotlight. The European war ended on the Seventh Army segment at Munich, Germany.

General Patch's report to General George Marshall was admirably brief. The Patch Board recommended a streamlined organization that was answered to their military occupational specialties was to incorporate a single department of the *Armed Air Forces* from the United States Army, and favored combining the Coastal Artillery (including the Anti-Aircraft Artillery) with the Field Artillery, forming an *Artillery Arm*. The horse had lost its usefulness on the battlefield. It was recommended that the Cavalry Arm be eliminated and be replaced by an *Armored Arm*. The United States Army Air Corps (USAAC) later became *United States Army Air Forces* (USAAF) to *United States Air Force* (USAF).

General Patch never lived to see those recommendations go into effect. He died in November 1945 at age 55 of pneumonia and, surely, a broken heart. His only son, Captain Alexander "Mac" Patch III, was killed at Épinal (Lunéville area) under his father's watch. Captain Patch III, also a West Point graduate, was with General Patton's Seventy-ninth Infantry Division when General Patch read in the paper that his son had been injured and hospitalized in England. Patch had his son brought to him to recuperate. While recuperating, the Seventy-ninth Infantry was transferred to General Patch's Seventh Army. A few days upon Captain Patch's return to action, he was killed. Mac's son (an only child) died in March of 1946. It was a sad ending to a dedicated general and the Patch name. He was all about his fighting men and keeping them safe.

General Patch talked with admirals and numerous leading military and naval personal and recommended that the armed forces be reorganized into a single cabinet department. The three coordinate combat branches—army, navy, and air force—comprise that operational service. The navy department opposed creation of a single department of defense and never did not acknowledge its own findings and continued to oppose the creation of a separate air force. Congress, at the recommendation of President Truman, created the department of the *United States Air Force* in September 1947.

In 1942, Harold Kristal enlisted and was sent to Kearns Air Force Base, Utah. In 1942, Kearns Air Base became a training field for Air Corps personnel. For three months, Harold went to X-ray School at Saint Louis, Missouri, and was assigned to the O'Reilly General Hospital, Springfield, Missouri. All the x-ray positions were filled, and Harold did hospital morning reports that no one else could do.

Harold was sent to Sheppard Field, a large training base in Wichita, Texas. He essentially repeated basic training that he had earlier at Kearns Air Force Base. He says the water tasted like oil—there were lots of oil wells around.

For more preflight training, Harold was sent to Big Springs, Texas, where aviation cadets were trained in high-altitude precision bombing as bombardiers. A small aircraft, AT-11 (Beechcraft Model 18), was their primary aircraft flown for training. They practiced with fifty-pound bombs made of tin filled with sand. Harold said they would sometimes hit oil wells with them.

It was in Ardmore, Oklahoma, at an overseas training unit, that Harold would meet Raymond Miller. In their training, Raymond learned as a copilot and Harold as a bombardier to fly in a B-17 Flying Fortress four-engine heavy bomber. Harold went overseas as a flight officer, which is the same rank as a warrant officer. At Deopham Green, they did combat formation flying practice on a large body of water on the coastline of Eastern England called the Wash. The Wash was an embayment of the North Sea; it was among the largest estuaries in the United Kingdom. The pilots and crewmen were being prepared for the chaos during a target mission and made them advance amid all the enemy fire ahead. After flying five more missions overseas, Harold was promoted to second lieutenant.

Harold's duty also required him to call for each crewman to put on his oxygen mask at ten thousand feet. From the flight deck, starting from the tail gunner to the front, he called every ten minutes to check on the crew until they returned to the ten thousand feet. Harold also was the gunner officer but says, "I never went to gunnery school."

After each flight mission, the guns were removed from the turret, and after they were oiled and cleaned, the gunners would report to the intelligence officer. In the aircraft, there is a pressure change. Harold said on one mission, a gunner had a toothache. He had a cavity, and the pressure change caused the tooth to ache.

On a mission to support the troops at the Battle of the Bulge, the crew at the back of the aircraft saw they were losing oil, so the pilots made a precarious landing at Merville Airport, a small airport in France. The rocker box cover had blown off the number three engine, and oil was spilling all over. They hadn't made it quite to the English Channel. They aborted the bombs and found out later in was on a farm in France. The stop was a safety decision, but the problem was minor. After staying overnight, the crew left the next morning. Harold said, "We got the day off."

The Merville Airport was built by Germans as a *Luftwaffe* airport as part of the defense of the Pas-de-Calais area. The USAAF engineers later converted the airport into an Allied airport. The British Royal Air Force used the airport as an advanced landing ground.

The scariest mission of Harold's thirty-five missions was on an early, foggy morning. The whole group of the three squadrons was flying, and with the weather obscure, they had to fly around the target. They had to find a place that was clear and landed at a British airfield at Wales, England. The aircraft was loaded with gas and bombs. The wind was coming from the left, and the aircraft came in slowly, drifting to the right, and continued to keep flying at low altitude, the Bombardier looking at the lighting system on the edge of each side of runway. They were as high as a fire hydrant placed on each side edge, unlike the United States embedded lights. They were very close to the Atlantic Ocean coming in on an angle. Hal said, "I was trying to get up higher and higher there in the glazed nose of the aircraft. I was speechless. Someone was saying, 'Harry, go around!'"

Harry had to make another run for it and finally landed the aircraft. They spent two or three days at the Wales British airbase. They were not used to women other than for a few Red Cross women. Each morning a female voice would say "Wakey-wakey!"

After an air crew had finished twenty-five missions they were allowed to go on what was called Flak Leave of Absence. Hal chose not to go to Scotland with the others and went on two other missions, and then he asked the commander to send him back with his regular crew with pilot 1st Lt. Harry Simmons and copilot 2nd Lt. Raymond Miller. Harry and Raymond flew their last combat mission on March 15, 1945.

First Lieutenant Harold Kristal still had two more missions to fly, and his last combat mission was on March 17, 1945, with a new crew. They almost crashed on takeoff. The weather wasn't as forecasted, and the pilot had to takeoff on instrument on an early, foggy morning. The pilot was going down the runway, trying to keep the aircraft straight, and realized he wasn't going straight and overcorrected causing the plane to wobble. The pilot finally managed to get the aircraft straight, and then it was all right. An unforgettable mission, but they made it back to base. They never saw any *Luftwaffe* fighters. The weather was such that they had to look around for *targets of opportunity* to abort the bombs. It was luck that the plane didn't veer off the runway and damage the landing gear.

Harold "Hal" Kristal chose to stay in the air force and found the air force separated from the army was much better. He would wear the army colors until 1949. He was no longer part of the "Brown Shoe Air Force." The army items and shoes were russet in color.

In 1947 to 1948, Harold took an administrative officers' course at Lockland Air Force Base in San Antonio, Texas. While in the hospital with a sprained ankle, he thought of getting out of the air force. It was at the time the Korean War was on the radar, and Harold decided to stay in the United States Air Force.

For four to five years, Harold was an instructor for the B-25 Mitchell American twin-engine medium bomber at Mather Airport, Sacramento County, California. The B-25 was used in 1942 during the Doolittle Raid on mainland Japan led by Lt. Col. Jimmy Doolittle four months after Pearl Harbor.

While stationed at Lowry Air Force Base at Denver, Colorado, Harold was assigned to radio target protection simulation. From Lowry Field, he was kicked out to (his non-favorite place) Sheppard Air Force Base, Wichita Falls, Texas, where he was assigned to intelligence. While at Sheppard Field, Harold wrote that he wanted out of intelligence and was sent to Korea in 1955 for one year as *adjutant administrative officer* in a squadron. The squadron people were aircraft maintenance people. While in Korea, Harold received his psychology master's certificate, which he had earned while assigned at Mather Air Force Base in California. He received his master's degree in school psychology at California State College which had a long tradition of excellent undergraduate and graduate programs in psychology. Harold had worked on his psychology degree for thirteen years.

With receiving his psychology certificate, Harold wrote another letter to be reassigned and, upon his return to the States, was sent back to Mather Air Force Base for one year. From Mather AFB, he went to Los Angeles Air Force Base in research, home of the Space and Missile Systems Center. It was here that Harold was introduced to missiles. Titan was moved from Los Angeles AFB to Norton Space and Aeronautics, San Bernardino, California-which had been closed but was reopened just for Titan.

The Thor sixty-five-foot-long missile was the first operational-range ballistic missile deployed by the USAF, a medium-range ballistic missile powered by a liquid-propellant rocket engine. It was too limited to launch from the United States. It was named after the Norse god of thunder.

The Titan liquid-fueled, strategic intercontinental ballistic missiles were part of the United States deterrent until 1980. They were used for United States military payloads as well as civilian agency intelligence-gathering satellites and were used to send highly successful interplanetary scientific probes throughout the solar system. Primary used by United States Air Force National Aeronautics and Space Administration. It was launched from California over the Pacific. The Titan had a long history of modification as the United States's expendable rockets used from 1959 to 2005.

Harold retired from Norton on June 30, 1963. His road to retirement after twenty-one years of dedication to the air force on June 30, 1963, found him finding new challenges. At Norton, he saw all these small airplanes and said, "Hot dog! I am going to learn to fly and get my private license."

Harold got his private certificate and commercial and instructor ratings. He bought his own plane, and to maintain his airplane, he got a mechanic certificate. Aircraft maintenance technicians (AMTs) inspect, perform, or supervise maintenance, preventive maintenance, and alteration of aircraft and aircraft systems. They are referred to as A and Ps, for airframe and powerplant mechanics. It took Harold one year each to get both his airframe and powerplant certificates. He taught flight aviation mechanics and later was an aviation inspector at the Santa Monica Airport before going to the John Wayne Airport, Santa Ana, California. For a short period, he had served as a recruiter. Harold Kristal retired with the rank of major in the air force.

Harold Kristal played cornet in different bands before going into the Army Air Corps. He has a real love for band and orchestra music and listens to it regularly. He played the bugle while in an *air force training detachment* using his own cornet without pushing on the values. Harold is still very active and attends a *music appreciation class* each week. A band has no stringed instruments while an orchestra does. Orchestra pieces, called symphonies, can last for a half hour or more, while bands do not play pieces of music longer than ten to fifteen minutes. Harold enjoys listening to and identifying stringed instruments (violins, violas, cellos, etc.) and bass and percussion instruments. Bands do not have stringed instruments like the violin and cello. He is a person who never had a handicap when it came to learning. Harold is very articulate—someone who still strives to learn.

Chapter 12

Warzend's Radio Operator

George Culnon, *radio operator and gunner* and member of Raymond's flight crew, had passed his exam test for the Air Corps. Upon entry, he was sent to Wright-Patterson Air Force Base five miles northeast of Dayton, Ohio, where he was assigned with the Air Corps maintenance group. It was here that George decided to try out for cadet training. He and one other person became replacements for a cadet who was leaving the program. From Wright-Patterson Air Base, George was sent to Tulare, California, for basic training. He began his basic flight training at the Tulare Rankin Air Field. The Tulare Field was owned and operated by Tex Rankin, who was a stunt pilot who demonstrated his pilot skills through intricate maneuvers.

The trainees did the regular basic training: running (a great deal) and quite a few programs for learning the remnant of flight, engine, maintenance, and repair, with actual flight training in a PT-17 Stearman. The PT-17 Stearman was the principal trainer used by the USAC in primary flight training. George had eight hours flying before he could solo. It was a very exciting moment for George, and he had very good flights in his solo position. He had previously ground looped two times, which had agitated the canvas repairman, and the man proceeded to tell George he should *fly in a more level position and not cause him to make all those repairs!*

George said, "There were six men in my crew, and they were all very nice young men. They called me Ace for some reason," and added, "I know I was a long way from being an Ace. They were great comrades."

They were assigned to one instructor, Mr. Billingsley, who was a fine gentleman and an expert pilot and very active with the men. Upon their arrival at the base, he had taken them to his home and made them feel welcome. In primary training in order to train the military pilots, most of the instructors were civilians who were very accomplished pilots. Mr. Billingsley did wear an army uniform, but wasn't connected with the army other than for a pilot instructor.

Most of the cadets were college-caliber people who were in college, ROTC, or had entered college by way of the army. George had applied for military service right out of high school in Steubenville, Ohio. He found there was a need for some college background for the classwork. He had no idea of quitting—just hoping and praying not to be eliminated. He would have been assigned to a college training detachment if he had come out of college.

While in California, George was lonesome. He excelled in sports, racing, running, and in speed performance of his assigned activities. He felt he was qualified but didn't have the polish or experience that college programs provided. George said, "I had to learn how to learn."

George went on to excel in identifying aircraft in one course and, in his machine shop work training, had a basic knowledge of the airplane, motors, and equipment that helped a little bit, but he still felt that he wasn't the best. His two ground loops in the program bothered him.

George enjoyed the acrobatics of the owner, Mr. Rankin. There were times when Mr. Rankin could barely hobble out to the plane to get in, yet he could fly like a bird. He was entertaining!

When George graduated from primary training, he had made a few other friends and flew his normal hours. He didn't ground loop after that because he didn't think the plane would ground loop that easily for he had more control of it. It was a much heavier airplane. He went on to advanced flight training and took a few more chances with more confidence in flying and thought, *Well, I am on my way, and I am going to make it*, until a rather reckless incident happen. George was flying the instrument panel and enjoyed that but got into a little scrape and wasn't as honest as he should have been. He was kicked out, and he said, "I was guilty and accepted that."

In the meantime, while awaiting the judgment of the committee that heard his case, he made friends with a link trainer and went through a complete training program with him. The trainer proclaimed George to be an excellent fighter pilot and recommended that George not be washed out, but he didn't have much clout. George says his attitude was not what it should have been for a military pilot. He had a check ride with a colonel to another air base. He returned to enlisted ranks and followed on from pilot to sergeant gunner and excelled.

George knew the guns well from his youth and had worked with guns. George was a very good marksman. He did real well in that category and went on to radio school. As a boy scout, he had learned Morse code, and that was important for a radio operator. He would go and made an excellent radio operator as a bomber crew member.

At Oklahoma, they were taught to fly in a B-17 four-engine heavy bomber specifically for overseas duty. They learned stopping engines, feathering the propeller, flying on three engines, transferring fuel, setting the instruments, and all the fine points of navigation. Feathering the propeller on a failed engine allowed the aircraft to maintain height with the reduced power from the remaining engines. Depending on the design, the pilot may have to push a button to overdrive the high-pitch stops and complete the feathering process, or the feathering process may be totally automatic.

George learned all the points of air-to-ground gunner and air-to-air gunner also. They spent several weeks at Ardmore, Oklahoma, learning to operate the B-17 Flying Fortress heavy bomber.

The crew was assigned to pick up a new B-17F at Lincoln, Nebraska, and fly the new airplane to England. They flew over the island of Greenland and on to Iceland, where their near-crash landing scared

George, and he thought that was *it* before they got overseas. When they landed in Iceland, they hit a wind curve that almost turned the plane over—it was tilted to that degree. It probably would have spun in, but it was such a heavy plane and received that strong wind current. The scare lasted only a few seconds, which seemed like an eternity. For the crew, it was just the beginning of some of the heroic experiences they would meet in their future assignments.

Lieutenant Simmons, the pilot in command, had flown them cross-country and told the crew that they were flying a route that he had posted and gotten permission for. He flew over his hometown of Chicago and over George's hometown of Wilton, West Virginia. George looked down at his home and told the others that it was where he lived—that was exciting moment for George.

The training of the heavy bomber program was designed to fit each member of the crew for the handling of his assigned job. It was imperative for radio operators to know all there was to know about the radio equipment. Lives depended on his ability in handling his job. Behind the bomb bay sat the radio compartment, the position of the radio operator, a technical sergeant in charge of the multiple radio communication and navigation devices onboard the B-17 heavy bomber.

George says for their mission, the crewmen were awakened at 3:00 a.m., got dressed, ate breakfast, and headed for the briefing room where they were advised where the mission would be and all the things that pertained to it. Everyone rode to their plane's point area and set up their battery of radios. They were not only monitored for transmitting but were told what to do, how they were to talk, and when to remain radio silent over the target or the continent. There was much to do, and it was very important that silence was maintained and the radio operator still be available when requested by the commander of the plane for weather, for other important information on the different air bases to land in, or different actions to take. It was a responsibility that was helpful to the mission. The radio operator also handled the chaff that had to be dispersed from the plane (which the air force used to interrupt the radar of the enemy to save their planes), observed the area closely and reported any incidence of any planes that were in danger of being too close, or other problems that developed on a mission. The radio operator also managed the right waist gunner, a flexible .50-caliber machine gun, out of top of his compartment. George was supposed to be credited for half the planes shot down, but said, "That didn't matter for each crew member had contributed to the missions."

Copilot Raymond Miller was critically injured on his second flight mission with an experienced crew and was in the hospital. Meanwhile, his own crew flew thirteen more missions while Raymond was in the hospital. Upon the crew's return from a mission, they would buzz the hospital to let Raymond know they were back safely, which they would catch a little flak for. The plane wings were hitting the tree tops and shredding the leaves and severing some branches. Some of the crew visited Raymond and would report back to the others how he was doing and when he could possibly return.

One of the thirteen crew missions was to the harbor where German naval gunners were assembled. The Germans would shoot at them, and the crew would return to base pretty ragged. At the navy ports, the gunners were considered better and more adequate shooters. There were some missions that they missed. Some went to Regensburg, Germany, and back to Berlin when they thought the Germans were on the run. Berlin was hit more often. On one mission, they crash-landed in Belgium, which was another heroic experience, not knowing who would greet them when they came out of the plane—if they were Americans under American control or not. They had no problems other than getting back from Belgium. They followed the routine schedule. Some missions were more difficult than others. On the first mission to Berlin, the aircraft was shot up fairly severely.

Frostbite was an enemy for all crews, and with the temperature at thirty-five thousand feet high or whatever areas of an extreme temperature, frostbite was always there to take its toll. George, for one, had an incident where he forgot his heating element for his suit and had suffered the consequence. He learned an important lesson that was probably passed on to the other crew members for it is very dangerous to be hit by frostbite.

On one mission, the bombs did not part the aircraft but jammed in the bomb bay. Flight Officer Harold Kristal (bombardier) requested for George Culnon to come into the bomb bay and assist him in the release of the bombs. Lieutenant Kristal was halfway in the bomb bay trying to release the bombs and needed assistance at the other end of the bomb bay to release the bombs. While Kristal was in a precise position on the catwalk with the bomb bay door open, the area was too tight for a parachute with all his other clothing. Officer Kristal handed George one riser from the harness, telling him to hang on for dear life. George lay on the central rail of the plane, holding on to the riser. After some time, Kristal got the bombs to release and asked George to call the pilot to close the bomb bay door.

There was an incident when George was hit by flak that broke the skin, but he never reported the incident and said, "It was such a minor hit, and I didn't feel like reporting it at the time, knowing what pain and agony the crew had suffered. It was OK, but now I see there may have been an advantage. In retrospect of seeing so many losing so much, I am glad I didn't." Raymond said that George should have applied for the Purple Heart.

George said their group didn't play much poker or drank too much. He had slowed down on his drinking. He drank before he went into the Air Corps. They had beer in England, and he thought that he had gotten hooked on their stout. The crewmen called *off and off* beer. He would go in at a pub and ask for their *off and off* beer and they would say, "You can talk better than that," and then set him up a great, big glass. The stout beer, a nourishing dark ale, was popular during World War II.

One day, George went to London and went through all the museums and saw three golf courses that he enjoyed. He was with two other crewmen who played basketball. One player would later play pro basketball. The three went to a London pub where they met a Russian sailor. George bought the sailor a beer, but the other two wanted to show off because they would fight together and gang up on one guy.

The sailor could speak some English and told George that he was a pretty nice guy. The two with George kept at the Russian, and pretty soon, the Russian turned around and beat the heck out of both of them. The two tried to get George to come in and help. George responded, "Do you think I am crazy? I am not going to take on a Russian champion!" The Russian just laughed and nudged George. The two crewmen left the pub, leaving George there. George and his Russian friend left the pub and walked for a long ways together. George continued walking all night. He had walked all afternoon the day before. George had to fly one more mission with a new crew and almost lost his life.

Chapter 13

Flight Crew's Duties

The duties and responsibilities depended on the flight crew's job of accuracy was vital to accomplish a successful mission and cannot be overemphasized for a weak link can result in the loss of the entire crew. During a time of conflict, civilian weapons and methods were found to be an advantage just as the military weapons.

In aviation, part of the navigator's duty as an instrument pilot was to use radio navigation aids. During their training, cadets learned the low-course range, but this only worked when flying navigation along one of the four ninety-degree radials related to the actual direction to the station till the signal increased or decreased in strength. To navigate, they had to be along the beam.

Navigation is to determine the plane's position relative to earth. The navigator also defended the plane using the cheek guns mounted in the nose section of the plane. The navigator navigated the plane using pilotage, dead reckoning, celestial navigation, and radio. The navigator's primary duty was navigating the plane with a high degree of accuracy, and he had to have general knowledge of the entire operation of the plane. He was to direct the flight from departure to destination and return and must know the exact position of the plane at all times.

The *flight engineer* was the crew member who was supposed to know more about the plane than any other member of the crew—the top turret, engine monitoring. He was the chief source of information concerning the airplane and was trained in the air force's highly specialized technical schools. He was an integrated crew member, positioned on the main flight deck just aft of the pilot and copilot, and worked in close coordination with the pilots during *all* phases of a flight. As airplanes became larger and more complex, the flight engineer aboard a flight was equipped with his own specialized control panel, allowing him to monitor and control the various systems, which helped with the pilots' workload, notably during takeoffs and landings.

On the way back home after a successful target mission and at a lower altitude and without their oxygen masks, flight engineer T/Sgt. Lynn Davis Jr. and Raymond Miller would enjoy a cigar. They were the only crew members who would smoke.

The *ball turret gunner* needed great eyesight to aim accurately and have great mental concentration. The ball turret gunner protected the aircraft from all enemy attacks coming from below. Curled up in the ball in a fetal position, with his back against the armor-plate door, he had less of his body exposed to enemy fire than other crewmen although he was hunched, legs bent, with his feet in stirrups on each side of the thirteen-inch-diameter armored glass panel.

Most Flying Fortress crew members considered the ball turret the worst position on the aircraft. The waist gunner helped the ball turret gunner into the Sperry ventral ball turret. The ball turret was very small in order to reduce the drag and was operated by the shortest crew member. To enter it, the turret was moved until the guns were pointed straight down. And then the gunner placed his feet in the heel rests and then crouched down into fetal position. He would then put on a safety strap and close and lock the turret door. With his back and head in midair by the two footrests on the turret's front wall, it gave him roughly eye-level position with the pair of light-barrel Browning .50-caliber machine guns that extended through the entire turret, and located to either side of the gunner. A cable was attached to the handle through pulleys to a handle near the front of the turret, with the cocking handles being closely located to the gunner for him to operate more easily. The small ammo boxes rested on the top of the turret, and the remaining ammo belts were stowed in the already-cramped turret by means of an elaborate feed chute system. A reflector sight hung from the top of the turret, positioned between the gunner's feet. The turret was directed by two hand-control grips with firing buttons. Hydraulics normally powered elevation and azimuth—with hand cranks available for backup. The left foot was used to control the reflector sight range reticle. The right foot was used to control the talk intercom switch.

On the B-17, the turret was close to the ground, yet there was enough clearance for takeoff and landing. The ball gunner never entered the turret until the plane was well into the air in case of landing gear failure. There was no room for a parachute, which was left in the cabin above the turret. Raymond Miller said, "The ball gunner only had about a minute to put on his parachute. If you had claustrophobia of a tight space this job would not be for you. The turret was stowed with the guns facing rearward, in the direction of the tail, for takeoff and landing. It would be hazardous for the gun to be downward when landing a plane."

The *Fortress waist gunner* windows provided enemy defense protection. The gunners had flak helmets, flak suits, and an armor plate contoured to the curve of the fuselage below the windows as their only protection from the flak and bullets. The gunners stood at their guns, where the rest of the crew were sitting or kneeling. Waist gunners incurred the largest number of casualties of all the Fortress crew positions. The waist guns were the important *defense feature* of the B-17 formations. He assisted the other crew members as needed. He was also responsible for checking the aircraft for damage and, when necessary, assisting the flight engineer with repairs while in flight.

The earlier Fortresses were without the Plexiglas covering the waist window behind where the gunners stood, but it was introduced on the B-17G. The guns were mounted to the inner frame of the windows and enclosed with a permanent Plexiglas covering. The gunners no longer had to stand in freezing slipstream conditions as in the earlier models.

Frostbite had been an issue for the waist gunners who stood near open windows, areas that were open to fifty-below-zero temperatures. If a crew member was injured in the aft section of the plane, the radio operator or the waist gunner applied first aid. The waist gunner would call out any enemy fighter that was destroyed or damaged, how many B-17s went down, and the number of chutes seen going down from the falling bombers. This benefited the navigator and radio operator at their briefing once back at base.

The *tail gunner* of the Fortress was the most important *defensive weapon* of the bomber. The tail gunners inflicted severe damage on attacking fighters from the rear. The last B-17 in the formation known as the tail-end Charlie, as viewed by the tail gunner, was often the first aircraft to be attacked by enemy fighters. The gunners in the rear of the airplane would assemble in the radio room for takeoff, and once the aircraft was airborne, they would take their combat positions. The gunner would take his parachute, crawl around the tail wheel, and take his position with his knees resting on padded supports and his legs doubled back.

The tail gunners first appeared on the B-17E Fortress. The early Fortress models had no defense armaments in the rear and enemy fighters found the aircraft to be very vulnerable. The B-17G model modified the tail gun area with a better angle of fire and increased visibility by using what became known as the Cheyenne turret.

Once the crew had finished their combat practice at Deopham Green and given their ranks, the mission crew members never changed until on December 13 mission. At that time, waist gunner S/Sgt. Jess Willoman checked out, and crew members dropped to nine. Copilot Raymond Miller returned on December 25, 1944, from his November 5, 1944, injury replacing his replacement. *February 22, 1945, mission,* 2nd Lt. Harold Kristal was replaced with togglier-gunner, T/Sgt. Alfred Zubilagao. *On February 23, 1945, mission,* Second Lieutenant Kristal was again replaced with togglier-gunner, Sgt. Lyle P. McAfee. Ball turret gunner S/Sgt. Roger L. Boman was replaced with S/Sgt. James B. Kuykendall, waist gunner S/Sgt. Donald J. McHugh was replaced with

S/Sgt. Leon B. Briggs, and tail gunner Ray W. Bromps was replaced with Sgt. Joseph W. Duhan. *February 25, 1945, mission,* the togglier-gunner was S/Sgt. William F. Lewis. *March 1, 1945, mission,* S/Sgt. Eugene W. Marshall was togglier-gunner. *March 5, 1945, mission,* S/Sgt. Vance P. Vrban was togglier-gunner. *March 8, 1945, mission,* Harold Kristal returned as bombardier. On the *March 10, 1945, mission,* 2nd Lt. Harold Kristal returned as bombardier with the new rank of first lieutenant Harold Kristal, and waist gunner S/Sgt. Leon Briggs was replaced with S/Sgt. Jacob Wagner. *March 11, 1945, mission,* navigator 2nd Lt. John F. Nortness returned with rank of first lieutenant Nortness, and T/Sgt. Cecil Vigil was togglier-gunner. *March 14 and 15, 1945, missions,* 1st Lt. Harold Kristal returned as bombardier. This was pilot Lt. Harry Simmons and copilot Raymond Miller's last assignment to fly a combat mission. Soon after, Raymond was given rank of first lieutenant.

For crewmen, to see other Fortresses flaming, exploding, and falling all around out of the sky was hard. Heavy flak bursting everywhere left the whole crew wondering, *Are we next?* There were times when they simply prayed aloud. Their courage and abilities challenged by the Nazi braggart, they dropped their peaceful pursuits and beat him at his own bloody game so magnificently, flying the skies day by day. There were conditions when they were sitting ducks. "But we never chose to turn back no matter how many aircraft were lost on a mission," said Raymond Miller. "On an early mission, there was a whole group of ten aircraft lost. It was thought to be twelve, but two aircraft came in."

After the crew's last mission together, everyone seemed to have lost track of pilot Lt. Harry Simmons's whereabouts. He was playing football at Syracuse University in New York before entering the Air Corps. He was from the Chicago, Illinois area. He was a tremendous pilot. He flew in a low-element squadron, and in flak offensives, he would stray a bit from formation to keep the flak from coming in on the plane and still be in the formation's straight and level path. He never got into trouble. It surely helped to save the lives of his crewmen. It got around to where it was said, "If you want to be safe, *fly with Harry.*"

Chapter 14

The Mighty 452nd Bombardment Group

During World War II, a popular patriotic song on the home front, "Coming In on a Wing and a Prayer," described the daily travels of US bombers returning to England after a raid on Nazi Germany. Shot full of holes from German antiaircraft flak batteries and fighter planes, causing inoperable engines, crewmen didn't want to bail out and become POWs. The lyrics describe the condition of a damaged warplane, barely able to limp back to the airfields in the English countryside. The lyrics were by Harold Adamson, and the music by Jimmy McHugh.

Those who did objectives were in a high-risk venture for wind can kill or they could be taken captive when an airplane was brought down by enemy aircraft. Flying over hostile territory, timing was everything. Soldiers on the ground were supported by deploying bombs on tactical and strategic targets.

A midair collision or fire onboard aircraft, crewmen couldn't fight back. Some air crewmen never had the chance to bail out. It struck fear in the hearts of the crewmen even more than the enemy. Of the 450,000 United States deaths in World War II, fifty thousand were attributed to air warfare. When a bomber was destroyed in the air, ten men died. The

Luftwaffe officers discovered that on average, it took twenty hits with 20-mm shells fired from the rear to bring the B-17s down. The B-17 was noted for its ability to absorb battle damage, still reach its target, and bring its crew back safely with severe gashes in its fuselage. B-17s were the American Army Air Force's key (backbone) bomber aircraft of World War II in Europe. The B-17s dropped a total of 571,460 tons of bombs on European targets alone, as well as shooting down huge numbers of *Luftwaffe* fighters. Combat effectiveness and political issues also contributed to the B-17s success.

The airfield at Deopham Green, near Norwich, England, was home to about fifty B-17s and B-24s with about 2,500 men who flew, repaired, serviced, and maintained the air operation. For every bomber at the field, there were thirty or more men who repaired the plane, loaded the bombs and ammunition, maintained the radios, cooked, did the laundry, worked the PX, and did the other duties required to keep the planes flying and the field operating as well—all essential to successful launching of the air strike during an offensive mission.

Allen Hamman's radio operator, James Debth, says, "We would not have made it without those hardworking and conscientious men. They made sure that everything was in good condition on the plane, right down to washing the windshield, before we left. Just before we were to fly one day, a tuning unit did not work on my liaison radio set. I just about panicked, but when I went to the waist door and told the mechanic, he grabbed the unit and sped off in a jeep to get another unit. He was soon back, and I installed the unit and was all set to go. The ground crew watched as we took off and was there when we got back, all the time sweating it out. If we had any damage, they would jump right on it to get it repaired. They asked if everything worked OK on the mission. We shared cigarettes with them. I was happy to because I didn't smoke. We had several different crews as we never knew which plane we would fly each day. Sometimes we would get the same plane."

It was not uncommon for ground crew to have to take their bare hands in subzero temperatures and wipe aircraft with ethanol. Glycol kept the aircraft deiced. The risk of frostbite was acute. The checklist the pilot and copilot would go through together before takeoff were preventive measures to prevent accidents of the planes. Raymond said none of his crew received any frostbite on his missions, but there were other crewmen who did.

All crewmen were in their very early twenties, and every crew member was a volunteer who flew very long missions, sometimes resulting in the unusual stress of flying under extreme cold, with a constant hum and vibration, and being exposed to enemy fighters and heavy flak. Their required *tour* was thirty-five missions before returning to the United States. In early 1944, the number of missions per tour had been extended from twenty-five to thirty, and then later, five more tour missions were added to make thirty-five.

After the bombardment group completed thirty-five missions, they earned membership in the exclusive Lucky Bastard Club. Eligibility was celebrated by the pilot giving the tower a *buzzy job* after completing his final mission, a dramatic low-level flyover of the home base at full throttle with a simultaneous burst of brightly colored magnesium flares spewed from the B-17 in an exuberant display of triumph. Of the flying squadrons that started with the 452nd in World War II, only the 729th remains, flying C-17s as an aircraft squadron. On March 1945, Raymond Miller entered the *Lucky Bastard Club.*

Chapter 15

Casualties of War

Most of the aircraft reached England ahead of the ground forces. The army's high command viewed the aviation arm as an auxiliary branch to support ground forces. They supported ground forces rather than independent operations. The bombers' group helped prepare invasions, struck coastal defenses despite vigorous fighter attacks and heavily flak, hit enemy communications in and near combat zones; they assisted the airborne attacks and bombed airfield in support of the airborne assaults. Raymond says, "One place that was never taken was Dunkirk."

In 1940, at the Battle at Dunkirk, the British forces aided the French. Encircled by the Germans, they retreated to the area around the port of Dunkirk. With the decision to evacuate Allied armies trapped in France and in the race against time, the British left behind a massive amount of military vehicles, equipment, and supplies. During the Normandy campaign, many of the Germans who escaped had retreated to Dunkirk. The town was heavily fortified and well supplied for a lengthy siege from the navy and air force. In the fall of 1944, the Allies attempted to retake Dunkirk. The ports were needed to supply the Allied armies. Under pressure from Allied Supreme Commander, General Eisenhower, General Montgomery modified his instructions to the Canadian commander for the forces assigned to capture Dunkirk to be released to assist on the Scheldt and open access to the port at Antwerp. Montgomery decided to contain the German garrison within Dunkirk without attacking the fortified city.

Of all the German fortress garrisons on the Channel coast, Dunkirk was to have been the most resilient on the eastern side. There had been a flurry of attacks and retaliatory counterattacks. After the German surrender, the garrison at Dunkirk surrendered unconditionally to Alois Liška on 9 May 1945.

The 452nd completed 250 total combat missions in Europe. In the European Theater, the 452nd Group flew their last missions on 21 April 1945. All those strategic aerial bombardment missions of military targets significantly reduced the enemy's industrial installation capacity and production. At the war's end, the 452nd's last missions from Deopham Green were humanitarian flights to Holland, where food drops were released to the starving, during Operation Chowhound in May 1945. Rescue missions were flown to liberate the British, French, Dutch, and American prisoners of war.

The whole crew was made up of specialists—each man was an expert in his line whoever he was. Raymond attributes the close camaraderie of his crew to the complexity and dangers of the bombing missions. Each crew member individually performed a difficult task to help crush the German tyranny and was blessed when the war was declared over in Europe. Each had enlisted in a whole single purpose to give common aid to try to restore all that is *good* and *decent* and *righteous* in mankind.

The 452nd Group had severe losses in its 250 missions. There were missions where the traffic pattern could be dangerous, and the zero-visibility weather they flew in was worse than the actual mission. There were many times when flight crews were in their aircraft, feeling elated to be flying home but shaky, too. The United States bombers were the best, but nothing compared to the power of the small group of crewmen who flew a B-17 aircraft.

The Eighth Air Force casualties exceeded those of the United States Marine Corps and the United States Navy combined. The air force worked with safety procedures and worked to keep it intact.

There are airmen from the 452nd Bombardment Group that are buried on foreign soil at an American military cemetery near Cambridge, England, among other GIs. The 452nd Bombardment Group lost Lt. Col. Herbert O. Wangeman, who became a POW. The 728th Squadron leader, commanding officer Captain George T. Oxrider was killed in action. Each had served nobly. One had given his life while the other served as a POW so that we may live the freedom we know. Those who came home had so much to be proud of. They gave for their country.

There were 250 missions flown by the 452nd Bomb Group with their intended targets. Antiaircraft fire and tons of ordnance were dropped, destroying and crippling Germany. It was not until late in the war that the Allies gained air superiority. The 452nd Bomb Group would be among the last of the B-17 heavy bomb groups to arrive in England at a most critical time of the war. It was as though they became the hand of God that had reached out to help bring inner peace and strength for our Allied freedom.

Chapter 16

Farewell to Air Corps

After March 15, 1945, First Lieutenant Raymond's and First Lieutenant Simmons's duties were done. The crewmen still had two flights to do. Raymond was kept on as duty officer, answering the phone. In May, Raymond was sent home for a thirty-day leave. From Liverpool, England, he was zigzagged back across the ocean on the SS *Ile de France*, a huge French ocean liner. The war was still on with Japan, so evasive action had to be taken from submarines all the way across the Atlantic. On 8 May 1945, while Raymond was on the ocean liner coming home, there was a blackout in celebration of the victory in Europe on 8 May 1945.

After thirty days at home, Raymond was sent to Santa Ana, California, where he was being trained to fly in the B-25, a light medium bomber, and was to be sent to the Pacific Theater. They convened one day and were told that pilots with enough points were to be discharged in July. Raymond, having accrued plenty of points, elected to take their offer. He was discharged in July 1945, before the war ended in Asia. It was an air force experience the young copilot Miller would never forget.

Returning home early, Raymond got to see that for four years, the United States people maintained a dedicated effort, many working long hours seven days per week to help the war efforts. The United States' manpower was the largest human effort in history—everyone played an important part. For Raymond, it was a humbling experience to see his homeland's loyalty and indomitable courage in the face of all-but-insuperable obstacles, and their unselfish cooperation in all areas helped the victory. Raymond very much refutes any heroic accolades for flying the famous B-17 Flying Fortresses into German territory. He feels he was given a job to deliver bombs and ammunition and saying it was "much like a truck driver who was delivering his company's product."

Raymond returned home in July 1945. His father was working the night shift at the Standard Oil Company, and Raymond went to see him. Raymond says, "He gave me a big hug. It was my observation at the time that was the first time that Dad had ever hugged me."

With money saved from his army pay, Raymond bought a 1941 Buick. He enjoyed being home and visited relatives and friends and played golf. He quickly found that he would need fuel stamps to keep driving.

One evening in 1945, Raymond and his mother and father were playing cards when there was a knock on the door, and as a greeting, Russell said, "Deal me in!"

Finally, messenger of peace, shortly after, Richard got home. As Raymond and Russell, Richard enlisted in the Army Air Corps and trained as a fighter pilot. The three Rs would fulfill their dream. To fly an airplane was something Raymond and his brothers had an interest in since boyhood. The Rs' interest in flying may have started when their father made them this huge kite out of newspaper, clothesline posts, binder twine for the string, and a pail of sand for the tail. Richard was trained and ready for overseas duty. He had a quiet resolve to see the job through and a fighting spirit as Raymond and Russell. For Raymond and Russell, during each of their flight missions, they knew they might not return. Three brothers were devoted comrades-in-arms who chose to serve in two military alliances, the war between Allies and the Axis. World War II was the most widespread war in history.

There were nine crewmen on the B-17G *Warzend*. The crew's positions and duties don't tell how much these young crewmen gave in combat, their anxious young minds acutely focusing as each member rode the jeep to the waiting airplane. They never let *what if* stand in their way, but they carried on with *what is*.

The first mission is a valuable learning experience, which is why a new pilot was placed with a veteran crew for his first two missions. The rigorousness of close-formation flying for long periods of time would place tremendous physical and mental strain on a single pilot. It was for that reason, it was essential for a copilot to take over to save the crew as well as the aircraft.

Raymond's brother, Russell Miller.

1st Lt. Raymond Miller Pilot

Ten-member crew of the 728th Squadron assigned to the 452nd Bombardment Group. *Top row, left to right:* Flight engineer Layman Davis, radio operator-gunner George Culnon, ball turret gunner Roger Boman, waist gunner John Sutter, waist gunner Donald McHugh, and tail gunner Ray Bromps. *Bottom row:* Aircraft commander Harry Simmons, copilot Raymond Miller, navigator John Nortness, and bombardier Harold Kristal.

The nine-member crew. *Top row, left to right*: First pilot Harry Simmons, copilot Raymond Miller, navigator John Nortness, and bombardier Harold Kristal. *Bottom row:* Lyman Davis, George Culnon, Roger Boman, Donald McHugh, and Ray Bromps.

Air tower at Deopham Green, England. A brick was taken from the Deopham tower and used to build an exact replica at Wright Patterson Air Force Museum in Dayton, Ohio.

Air control room.

1st Lt. Raymond Miller Pilot

Briefing room of a mission.

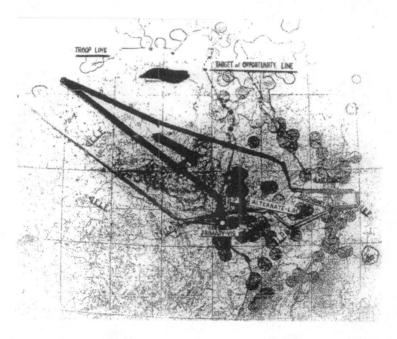

Intelligence photo: Photo shows route in, primary target, alternate target, secondary target, and target of last resort.

B-17s—hit in front.

In formation for protection against the German fighter aircraft.

1st Lt. Raymond Miller Pilot

Dodging flak.

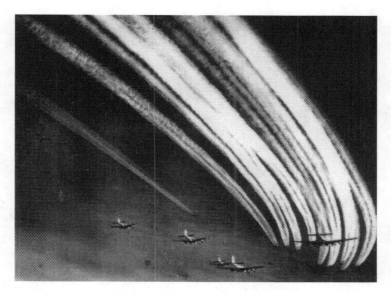

Vapor trails.

Dropping bombs on target.

Boeing US B-17G Flying Fortress heavy bomber.

1st Lt. Raymond Miller Pilot

Left to Right: Copilot Ray Miller (masked), flight engineer Lyman Davis, and pilot Harry Simmons in the cockpit of *Warzend*.

On a mission to Hanover, Germany. Navigator John Nortness and Raymond Miller are in the cockpit of *Warzend*. John is holding the large piece of shrapnel that came through the nose of their B-17 in his left hand just below the hole.

On November 5, 1944, 1st Lt. Allen Hamman was the second veteran pilot (required of two flight missions) that Raymond Miller would fly with before he could fly on his own mission.

Allen Hamman's flight crew. *Back row, L-R:* Joe Botta, engineer-upper turret; Amber Sutherland, bombardier; Allen Hamman, pilot; and Bud Paulsen, navigator. *Front row L-R:* Herb Rustad, tail gunner; Art Lovrien, left waist gunner; and Jim Debth, radio operator-right waist gunner

1st Lt. Raymond Miller Pilot

Jim Debth departing from plane. Last mission on January 8, 1945.

Shell hit left tire—20-mm shell. Raymond Miller said they were lucky to have landed the plane safely.

Shell hit the plane's wing.

2-mm shell in ball turret.

1st Lt. Raymond Miller Pilot

Hole from 2-mm shell in left waist and right waist gunner was hit and blew the floor out.

Shell went through the top of plane and upper turret.

The Air Corps picked Raymond's crew as the typical American bomber crew serving in England. They were sent to an English air base, and the British in turn sent their typical crew to the American air base.

Certificate given Raymond for entrance into the Lucky Bastard Club after he had completed the required number of missions—March 15, 1945.

1st Lt. Raymond Miller Pilot

B-25 light medium bomber.

Medals are Raymond's Air Medal and Purple Heart. The two pieces of metal are shrapnel that were removed from Raymond's chest on November 5, 1944.

Western Union telegram that Raymond sent to his parents from Santa Ana, California, saying, "Will see you soon. Love, Raymond."

Chapter 17

Brothers' Home

Once home, Raymond Miller hung up his pilot skills but would never forget. He would quickly pick up his love of sports again. Along with Russell, they played softball on the church team. One night, after playing a game on a hot evening and everyone had gone to bed, Richard had convulsions. As the family thought, the doctor confirmed that Richard had drunk too many soft drinks too fast. He recovered, not to remember having convulsions.

At the time, Raymond played on a championship softball team, and they had a pitcher who was famous all over the state. Before joining the team, Raymond was told the pitcher was so fast that he couldn't hold him. Raymond chose to challenge that by catching anything Hoke Wilson could throw. His team went on to win many tournaments and was a well-renowned softball team throughout the state of Indiana.

Raymond had played on several top teams in the area including the Marion Eagles, the American Legion, and the OnIzers. He was an outstanding receiver on the tough OnIzer squad, and exceptionally good behind the platter. Also a star backstop on the softball diamond, Raymond performed during the spring of 1945 as a member of the Marion All-Star softball aggregations and the powerful Marion Machine nine, which had been annexed to the Grant County championship tournament and the sectional title. During that time, Raymond became noted for his calm handling of erratic hurlers and was one of the leading hitters on the Gas City squad.

Raymond Miller was a capable backstop for the Gas City OnIzer baseball club, and regarded by many as the best catching prospect in the area and asked by officials of the Chicago Cubs, a National League club, to report for the 1946 spring training at Catalina Island, California, following a tryout with the Cubs at Wrigley Field, Chicago. Raymond was discharged from the United States Army Air Corps in the spring of 1945 after more than three years in service. During his three years' service time, Raymond played on several army air base nines, including the Randolph Field squad, National Service champions.

"It was a lot of fun." Catcher Raymond Miller on the baseball team said after his return from trying out for the Chicago Cubs. Raymond said that he participated in a four-inning practice game while Cub men watched. He didn't lose out altogether in the try out, having been made an offer to come back again next spring.

Raymond was also playing baseball at the time for the Owens-Illinois Glass Company's team. For Raymond, his life's plans were changed when the Owens-Illinois personal manager asked him if he wanted to come back to work for them. Raymond never knew at the time that he would have a rather long career with Owens-Illinois after getting a college degree. Raymond graduated from the Ohio State College of Education with majors in math and general science. He had signed a contract to teach in a secondary school in Evanston, Illinois, but before his graduation in 1951, a representative from Owens-Illinois came on campus and asked Raymond to come work with them as a project engineer. He chose to rejoin Owens-Illinois and worked as a combustion engineer and project engineer.

On September 9, 1955, the Industrial League Softball Team easily carried away the championship. The victory cup was presented to softball team captain Raymond Miller.

Raymond's brother, Russell, went to Ball State and received a degree in education and taught school and served as principal and superintendent at Marion, Indiana. He was principal at Terre Haute,

Indiana, and taught at Wabash, Indiana. After a three-year illness, Russell died in 1997. While stationed in Colorado for gunner training, he contracted Lyme disease, a bacterial sickness transmitted by a tick, and was very ill. Russell went ahead to Asia where he loaded the gunnery on aircraft.

Before going into the Air Corps, Richard graduated from the John Herron School of Art in Indianapolis, Indiana. Later, he opened and operated a successful advertising business in Indianapolis, Indiana. Richard died in 2005.

CHAPTER 18

A Personal Thank-You

In 2008, Raymond's son-in-law, Lee Moorman, took Raymond to the 452nd Group reunion held in Council Bluffs, Iowa. It was Raymond's first time to attend the group reunion.

During World War II, it was a usual practice for a new pilot to fly their first two missions with a veteran, experienced crew to introduce them to combat conditions. On his second mission, Raymond was assigned as copilot with 1st Lt. Allen Hamman and his crew. The second target mission was to Ludwigshafen, Germany, Raymond was severely injured. He had never known the name of the pilot and his crew who'd *chanced all* to save his life with an ultimate sacrifice. It was by the efforts of the group reunion staff and Raymond's son-in-law, Lee Moorman, that he was given the chance to know and thank Allen Hamman personally.

At the reunion banquet, it just so happened that Raymond and Allen Hamman sat next to one another, not realizing they had flown pilot and copilot together on November 5, 1944. Their name tags would not have identified anything for either one because they never knew each other's name. It was the policy of the air force crew members not to get to know one another, knowing the high-risk mission factor.

Lee took Raymond to Lt. Col. Allen Hamman's home in North Little Rock, Arkansas, so Raymond could thank Lt. Col. Allen Hamman and his crew after some sixty-four years. Raymond and Allen reminisced about some of their missions. Raymond asked Allen what he thought of those greenhorns who were being sent overseas, and Allen said, "That was me six months earlier."

Colonel Hamman and Raymond talked and shared stories of their missions. Allen told how, on his first mission with a veteran crew, they flew somewhere over France. They took off on controls, flying to join formation, and flew the airplane and dropped their bombs and turned around and starting back when the pilot turned the control over Allen. He was flying along when the pilot reached over in his pocket and took out a big chew of tobacco, and in Allen's mind, he wondered, *Where is he going to spit that stuff?* The pilot was paying no attention, just enjoying his relief, and reached up and pulled open the window and spit. Of course, the suction scattered it all down the side of the airplane. About every ten minutes or so, he'd pull open the window and spit. Allen thought, *My word, who would have thought of that. He could have had a can along or something to spit in.*

On one mission, they got hit by fighter planes when they were making an approach from the northeast with about one-hundred-knot tailwinds and their aircraft went whistling across there. Allen said, "We had to turn and go back out the same route that they came in, and at that point and time they were only doing seventy-five to one hundred mph on the ground, so those fighter planes could catch up with you really quick. I remember looking out and saw this one fighter plane go past, stop real still, putting on his flaps because we could be seen, and he could sit there in formation, firing. We lost six planes on that mission—sixty people. The losses were heavy."

On the December 24, 1944, mission, Allen Hamman just happened to draw the camera gunnery ship mission—no guns, just cameras. The mission was near the end of his tour of duty.

After his World War II tour ended, Lieutenant Hamman returned home and signed up for the Army Corps reserve and attended meetings once a month on weekends and took a course in correspondence. When the Korean War began, they recalled the whole reserve wing and individually picked who they wanted. Allen was sent to Japan, and while he was there, it was decided that they needed B-17 pilots, and Allen was reassigned. He flew back and forth to Korea on assignments. Allen smoked cigars and was teased about how many cigars he smoked while flying to Korea and back to Japan.

Allen worked in intelligence, and his assignments are unknown. His many assignments were to the Philippines, Guam, Thailand, and Vietnam. The last two years Lt. Col. Allen Hamman was in the air force, he was stationed in Washington DC. To keep his flying license up, he would go to Boeing Field near Seattle, Washington, on weekends to get the flying hours needed.

At the air force base in Little Rock, Arkansas, Allen spent ten years as director of the retiring activities office that he had started. He volunteered his time there and one day a week at the Little Rock Air Force Base pharmacy for the next thirty-four years. Lieutenant Colonel Hamman lacked ten days to having spent thirty-five years with the United States Air Force. Among his medals are two Distinguished Flying Crosses. Allen, 90, passed away January 2012.

Raymond got to meet a few of Allen Hamman's crew members at the 452nd Group reunion. Raymond never got to meet bombardier Lt. Amber G. Sutherland or engineer T/Sgt. Joe Botta, for both had passed away. Sutherland had been a VMI, which consisted of twenty-five cadets who pursued a four-year course of study. Sutherland's chosen course was medicine, and he later trained as a bombardier, which was a lucky omen for Raymond.

Lieutenant Sutherland had cared for crew member James "Jim" Debth during an October mission. James spent six weeks in an England hospital before returning to his flight crew. The day, October 5, 1944, would be a mission to remember for James Debth. James generously shared a few of his B-17 stories for Raymond's book. Raymond Miller was fortunate to meet James and Arthur Lourien at the 452nd Group reunion in 2008. Raymond, James, and Arthur were all assigned with the 728th Bomb Squadron. Arthur Lourien was the left waist gunner on Allen Hamman's aircraft. He was the youngest member of the crew. He was on the flight mission to Ludwigshafen when Raymond was injured and added, "I knew what was going on as bombardier Lieutenant Sutherland took care of Raymond Miller, but I was at the back of the plane."

Amber Glazebrook Sutherland of Virginia, at age 81, died April 2001. Sutherland was a retired chemistry professor and taught in the Clifton Forge school system and the Dabney S. Lancaster Community College, in Clifton Forge, Virginia. His medical knowledge along with Joe Botta's quick thinking saved Raymond on that Sunday of November 5, 1945.

James Debth said they called all the airplanes they flew in with Allen Hamman *Mr. Completely*. With them being a replacement crew, the planes had previously been named by a former crew. James Debth, radio operator and gunner, and the left waist gunner, Art Lovrien, are the only living men of Lieutenant Colonel Hamman's crew. The crew always looked up to and admired pilot 1st Lt. Allen Hamman whom they called Ham. James Debth says, "Allen was the best!"

Young Debth was inducted into the service on March 8, 1943, and assigned to Atlantic City, New Jersey, for his basic training. After six weeks, he was scheduled to ship out with his class. Upon his morning physical report to ship out, he had a 103 temperature and was sent to the hospital. They thought he had measles. After a week, he was sent to the main hospital, which was Haddon Hall, a large hotel on the Boardwalk. There he was diagnosed with scarlet fever. He spent a total of forty-five days in the hospital.

Upon James's hospital dismissal, he was sent to his next assignment, which was Scott Field, Illinois. It was a radio school. He was there for twenty-two weeks, learning Morse code and how to send and receive it on a transmitter at fifteen words a minute. He also had to learn radio mechanics and how to use a radio. After graduating from radio school, he was sent by rail to gunnery school in Yuma, Arizona. Their training started with learning about .50-caliber machine guns. They were taken out on the range to skeet shoot so they could learn to lead on a target. Later they would shoot the .50-caliber machine gun at a target. The gun was mounted on a pedestal. Finally, they were taken up in a plane to fire at a tow target from another plane. They also learned how to fieldstrip the machine gun, taking it apart and putting it back together blindfolded. They graduated after six weeks, and James was promoted to sergeant. From there, he shipped out to Salt Lake, Utah, where they made up the crews. James was placed with pilot Allen Hamman.

James says,

>From Salt Lake City, we were sent to Dalhart, Texas, where they started us flying in the B-17 Flying Fortress bomber for what was called phase training. We would all practice our skills and getting in formation with other planes. We spent two months in Dalhart and were sent to McDill Air Base in Florida by rail. We would spend another month or so finishing up our training. As we left McDill Field, we would travel by train to a port where we boarded a ship to cross the Atlantic. We had to walk a long way with our luggage to the *Aquitania* ship. It was a sister ship to the *Lusitania*, which was sunk sometime earlier. Not a good start, we thought. The ship was British and they sent us down to G deck, which was at the bottom of the ship. We had a very unpleasant seven-day trip, landing in Glasgow, Scotland. Date of departure, June 15, 1944. Date of arrival, June 22, 1944.

>We boarded a train and headed for our base, we thought. On the way, they stopped to drop off all the radio operators. The place was called the Wash. The radiomen would get more training for air-sea rescue operations and procedures, learning how to operate a new high-frequency radio for the planes to use on our missions. We were in class all day for six days, and then we took an exam on the seventh day. They told us that if we didn't pass, we would be taken off the crew.

We learned that all the assistant radiomen were to be taken off all the crews and would be flying medium bombers. We had to say good-bye to our assistant, Jack Rentz.

Finally we made it to Deopham Green base, which was the 452nd Bomb Group. We were assigned to the 728th Squadron and part of the Third Air Division. I was promoted to tech. sergeant, which was my last promotion in service.

August 26, 1944

We flew our first mission to Brest, France. We were a part of thirty-two replacement crews that were sent over. We were awakened at 3:30 a.m. An orderly came down the boardwalk, stuck his head in the front door of the hut, and said, "Botta, you are flying."

Joe was head of the enlisted men, and it was his job to get all of us up and out to fly. We would jump out of bunks, get dressed, and hurry out to catch the truck that would take us to mess hall. If we missed it, we would have to run all the way. We had powdered eggs, juice, and toast for breakfast. We then ran out to catch the truck that would take us to the supply room near the briefing room. There we would pick up our gear to fly—headed suits, parachutes, flak suits, radio information, oxygen masks, etc.

We then went to be briefed on the mission we were to fly. All the crew members would take a seat in the briefing room and wait for the briefing officers to come in. Suddenly, someone would shout "Attention!" and we would all jump up until the officer told us to be seated. The officer would tell us how important the target was for the day. The map at the front of the room was covered, and when the officer would pull the cord holding the cover, we heard a lot of groaning from the crews that had been there.

We heard what the weather would be at the target and how heavy the flak would be and the number of possible enemy fighters. We learned that the information could change, but they did their best for us. We all got information to take with us. For me, it was the code of the day, frequencies for three radios I must tune up, etc. They had us synchronize our watches. We left the briefing room and caught the truck for the hardstands where our plane was. We got aboard the plane and went about our duties. The pilot went over his checklists with his copilot. The navigator, bombardier, and the engineer checked out their lists. The gunners installed their .50-caliber guns, and after I installed my right waist gun, I proceeded to tune all the radio equipment. Nothing was left to chance. Oxygen systems were checked to see if they were working because they would be very important for safety.

We then waited for the green flare to be fired from the tower, which meant that we could go. We taxied out to the runway where we were to take off. We were behind several other planes that were going to fly with us. There were twenty or more from our bomb group, depending on the target. Missions could be as long as eight hours (Berlin). Takeoff time was by 7:00 a.m. and we returned sometime later, depending on the mission.

The takeoff was an experience. The pilot taxied to the end of the runway and squared the plane. He then set the brakes and revved up the engines, released the brakes, and we were on our way. We moved very slowly down the runway as we usually had a maximum bomb load or more.

1st Lt. Raymond Miller Pilot

We kept looking out the window to see if we were airborne. We felt the plane rise slightly and then settle, then bounce, and we were in the air. We breathed a sigh of relief. Some of the planes didn't make it into the air on some missions. The pilot found the rest of our formation by checking the colored flares that were shot from the leaders, and we headed for the target. We gradually gained altitude and finally got to ten thousand feet. The pilot notified us, and we put on our oxygen masks. The formation increased the altitude until we reached thirty-five thousand feet, which was the altitude we were to use that day for the bombing. We flew to the target. Once we were on the bomb run, we could not take evasion action. We received a lot of flak at the target. I had packets of chaff, which was aluminum foil in strips, to throw out of the side of the plane. These were to foul up the enemy radar so that the flak would miss us. I don't know how well it worked because we still got plenty of the flak. We headed for home in formation so we would have protection from the fighters. The enemy fighters liked to catch the stragglers and shoot them down. The fighters would attack us before the target area and after the bomb run. Upon our return from the mission, we went to the gun shop to clean our gun barrels, even if we didn't use them. Then we headed for the debriefing room to tell the officers what we had seen.

We flew one day as a relay plane. The bomb bay was loaded with radio equipment. We would fly along the coast of Europe and relay messages back to headquarters from the group. The pilot, copilot, navigator, engineer, and radio operator were the only ones to fly. We didn't get credit toward our missions.

October 5, 1944

This was our tenth mission. We were awakened at the usual 3:30 a.m. time. We rolled out of the sack and caught the truck to the mess hall. After a delicious breakfast, we caught the truck for the briefing room. This would be a day for me to remember, although I didn't know it at the time. The briefing officer greeted us with the information that we were going to bomb Handorf, Germany, that day. The original target was supposed to be Münster but was changed. We were to bomb the marshalling yards. We had the usual preparation and, as usual, a full bomb load. The takeoff was again scary. We found our formation and were off for the target. As we approached the target, the flak was very thick. The bombing run went OK, and we dropped our bombs. We headed for home, and the flak kept coming. The pieces were flying all over the radio room, and I hunkered down at the radio desk in my flak suit. All of a sudden, I felt something go through my right leg and knew I was hit by flak. The piece continued on through my tuning units hanging on the back wall of the radio room and out the other side of the plane. I don't know how big it was. I called the pilot on the intercom and told him I was hit. He had the waist gunner to check me out, and then he told bombardier, Sutherland, to go back and see how I was. Sutherland had studied premedicine and knew what to do. He came through the bomb bay and saw that I had a piece of flak go through my right calf. There was very little loss of blood as the temperature was thirty-five degrees below zero and all the blood vessels constricted. He poured sulfa in the wound and gave me a shot of morphine. Then he bandaged my leg and wrapped a blanket around it so I wouldn't get frostbite. After making sure I was OK, both crewmen returned to their duties, watching for fighters.

1st Lt. Raymond Miller Pilot

We had several hours to go to reach our base, so I just stayed on the floor of the radio room. On the approach for landing, the crew shot off red flares until they ran out of them, and then they shot some green flares, hoping the ground crew would know that we had wounded onboard. The pilot landed the plane so smoothly I didn't know we were down. As we came to a stop, the medics were there right away, and the flight surgeon came onboard. He looked at my leg and gave me a shot of morphine, and I was carried off to an ambulance and headed for the hospital. Arriving there, they operated on me, giving me a shot to put me to sleep. The next thing I knew, someone was sitting by my bed, slapping me in the face. He said they had given me too much anesthetic, and he was to keep me awake as soon as I woke up. I spent about six weeks in the hospital and rehab. Meanwhile, my crew kept on flying while I was out of commission. When I returned to the base, I asked the pilot, Lt. Allen Hamman, if I could return flying with the crew. He arranged for me to rejoin them again, and I was glad because I had trained with them and had been flying with them.

Upon our arrival at Deopham Green base, we were assigned to a half-round Quonset hut of metal. It was about thirty feet long and ten feet wide, and housed two enlisted men crews of ten. It had a stove in the middle, which was to keep us warm. The hut had no installation. We received one bucket of coke to burn each day. We managed to borrow some more coke from the fenced-in yard. One person would climb over the fence and throw some coke back while someone watched for someone coming. To start the coke in the stove, we would stuff it with paper and then throw a flare in and quickly put the top on the stove. The colors of the flare would shoot out of the chimney.

When flying and returning to the hut, we would grab some clean clothes, a towel, some soap, and head for the shower. It was quite far. The building was made of concrete with wide-open windows. If you got there early, you might have some warm water. If not, the water was cold. We would jump in the shower, wash up, and dry off with the towel very quickly. Then we would run for the hut. The mess hall was always closed when we got back from our mission, so we would borrow some food from the mess hall—when we were there—and try to fix it on our stove. We would peel some potatoes and fry them in a pan we had borrowed. We went to bed early because we might be flying in the morning. Our sleep was interrupted by buzz bombs that were fired from the European continent by the Germans. Also, they sent rockets. When those exploded, the ground would shake for a mile. We were supposed to run into the shelters they had, but after a while, we learned that as long as we could hear them, it was OK. If the motor shut off when it was near, we would have to worry because they would immediately fall and explode.

We slept with about four blankets to keep warm. At one point, they asked us to give some of them up because they needed them for the front lines. We gladly gave some of them to the guys who needed them. Somewhere in between all this, we managed to keep our clothes clean, write letters, and do other things.

Once a month, we would get a two-day pass on a rotation schedule. If a crew went home, we would move up on the list. We all usually went to London by train. All the enlisted men would go to the nearest pub and we would have a drink. We would all take off for whatever we were to do while on pass. The engineer and I would go together and rent a hotel room. He and I would go sightseeing and get something to eat. Joe would decide to do something on his own, so we would go and do different things. We would meet back at the hotel and sleep through the night. Sometimes, his night was short because he would get in rather late. I always kept one ear out for him to come in. When I heard the door open, I would say "Is that you, Joe?" He would say "Yeah, Jim, it's me." Then I could sleep well. There was one time we moved up on the schedule and nobody had any money. I happened to have eighty-one pounds saved. A pound was equal to four dollars American money. I told the crew I would lend them all nine pounds each and they agreed to pay me back on payday. I sent the money home the next payday by money order.

December 5, 1944

Again, at 3:30 a.m. there were footsteps on the boardwalk outside F (our hut). The door opened, and a GI said, "Botta, you are flying."

We jumped out of our bunks, got dressed, and hurried to catch the truck to the mess hall. After a quick breakfast, we hurried to catch the truck to pick up our gear and head for the briefing room. When the briefing officers showed up, a silence fell over the group. The officers told us how important the target was for today, how much flak there would be, and how the weather was over the target. Then the briefing officers pulled the cover off the map on the wall, and we saw we were going to *Ludwigshafen, Germany.* There were gasps from the ones who had gone there before and a lot of grumbling. The officer said, "Good luck, men!"

We all synchronized our watches. Then I, as the radio operator, was told what frequency to use for the day and the code for the day. From the briefing room, we caught the truck to the plane we were flying that day. When we arrived, we proceeded to do whatever job was ours. The gunners all put their .50-caliber guns in the mounts. I put in the right waist gun and then I tuned the pilot's command set to the proper frequency, and next, the high-frequency set got tuned. From there, I tuned up my liaison set, which was used to send codes in case of an emergency. All the while, the bombardier was checking his settings for the bomb drop when we got there and the navigator was checking his maps, and all were going over the information given them at the briefing.

The pilot and copilot were doing the check of the instruments with the help of the engineer, who had installed his twin .50-caliber guns in the upper turret. The rest of the crew was checking the intercom and oxygen system. Nothing was left to chance. Then we waited for the green light flare from the tower, which meant it was a go for the mission. We taxied out to the runway behind the other planes that were already there ahead of us. When it was our turn, the pilot lined up with the runway, set the brakes, and revved up the engines, released the brakes, and we slowly crawled down the runway. We watched to see if we were going to make it airborne or not because we had more than a full load of bombs that day and two thousand gallons of gas. We were lucky today, as we made off the ground. We then circled and found our group to get in the proper place in the formation. After the group was formed, we were finally on our way. After a short time we were at ten thousand feet and had to put our oxygen masks.

As the radio operator, I had to monitor the radio in case we got a change from headquarters for the mission. As we crossed the English Channel, we picked up our fighter escort, which consisted of P51s and P47s. They would escort us part of the way until they ran low on gas, at which time they would pick out targets they could hit on the ground, and then head home. Later on, they used drop tanks—belly tanks—for extra gas, which allowed our fighter protection to follow all the way.

We cruised along at about thirty thousand feet and then got up to thirty-five feet before we got to the target area. We were picking up flak but didn't see a fighter yet. We finally reached the target, and the flak was intense and tracking. Once on the bomb run, we couldn't change our heading as we were locked in until we dropped our bombs.

After dropping the bombs, the group took a preassigned heading for home. We stayed tight together for protection from fighters, which we were starting to see. I signed off the radio to man the right waist gun, and everyone was firing now. All the time we were on the bomb run, and during the mission, we had oxygen checks to see if everyone was OK. The temperature was thirty-five below zero, and we had our heated suits on to keep us warm. We were hit pretty heavy with a lot of flak and also with 20-mm shells from their fighters. We had 20-mm shell hits in the right and left waist positions, one through the upper turret, one through the ball turret, one in the right tire, one in the right wing. The one that hit in the left waist shredded the bag of extra equipment, but that bag saved the gunner from losing his legs. The one that hit in the right waist, where I was, blew out the entire floor beneath me. We had engine troubles and had a hard time keeping up with the group. We lost one of the engines and shortly after, lost another one. We made it back to the English Channel and started to throw everything of weight overboard to lighten the plane—flak suits, extra equipment, gun barrels, and even the ball turret. We had to feather another engine. By this time I was back on the radio because the navigator needed a fix so we could head back to the base. I contacted the stations along the English coast with a CHIPT message that we were supposed to use and got the fix, which gave us a heading to the proper base, and relayed it to him. It was a good thing I contacted the coast because we were flying pretty close to London, and they would have shot us down as an enemy plane.

We finally landed at an emergency field where they guided us to, and they had to tow the plane off of the runway. Our pilot and copilot did a fantastic job of getting us home. We ended up with more than one hundred 200-mm shell holes in our plane.

We had to wait for several hours for them to send a truck to transport us back to our base. We arrived back at the base about 8:00 p.m. One good thing—we didn't have to clean our guns, as they were at the bottom of the English Channel.

After getting back to the base, we headed for the hut and scrounged around to find something to eat and then went over to the great shower building with open windows and cold water to take a shower and run like heck back to the hut for a good night's rest.

We thought we would not have to fly the next morning, but we were wrong. At 3:30 a.m. we were awakened and told we would fly. We all rolled out and headed for the usual routine of briefing and preparing to go to our next target.

1st Lt. Raymond Miller Pilot

January 8, 1945

It was 3:30 a.m. and footsteps were heard coming down the boardwalk. I jumped out of bed and got dressed to catch the truck to the mess hall. I was just a little concerned this day as I would be flying with a new crew. My crew has finished their tour of duty. After eating breakfast, I caught the truck to the briefing room. There I met the crew I was flying with that day. All of them were new except the engineer, who had flown before.

The briefing officer entered the room, and we were told that we would be bombing the marshalling yards at *Hoblenz, Germany*. We were told to expect moderate flak and the target could be overcast. After briefing, we all headed for the plane we would be flying today. It was time for us to install our guns and for me to tune up all the radio equipment. I installed my right waist gun and began my work on the radios. The left waist gunner could not get his gun to work and the tail gunner also had trouble with his guns. I thought this was not a good start for a mission. The green flare was shot from the tower, which meant we were on our way. We taxied out to the runway and made a good takeoff. We joined our formation and headed for the coast of Europe. We made it to the target in good shape with a lot of flak shot at us. We dropped our bombs and headed for home.

Fifteen of our aircraft were damaged and one aircraft was seen to have dropped out of formation with engine trouble. They were not seen again. The temperature this day was fifty-eight degrees below zero. As we got over the coast of England, we became lost and the sky was overcast and there was a lot of fog. We were too low for me to get a fix. All I was getting was a lot of static. We kept on flying around, and all of us were looking to try to see the ground. As I looked out of my radio room windows, I saw a hole in the clouds and called the pilot. He turned the plane around and headed for a field that we saw. We made a good landing without too much gas to spare. The pilot taxied to the headstand and cut the engines. We were back safe.

I secured my radio information and proceeded to the side door after removing my gun barrel to be cleaned. As I slid out of the door I was shocked to see my former pilot, Lt. Allen Hamman, and engineer, Lt. Joe Botta, standing there. That was when I found out that we had landed at our own base out of all that we could have landed at. They both welcomed me with open arms and Lieutenant Hamman said, "I have some good news for you. You have flown your last mission. You have flown twenty-five missions and fulfilled your tour." The commanding officer said, "You can go home now."

Finally, for James Debth, the war was over. James says, "I thanked the Lord and kissed the ground."

It was about two weeks later, James was assigned to return to the States on a hospital ship with other returnees in order to help with the injured GIs who were in casts and disabled. They would take them their meals and carry them on deck for boat drills. With the war still on in Europe, they traveled in a convoy that took fourteen days crossing the Atlantic. The Statue of Liberty site really looked great when the ship pulled into the New York Harbor February 24, 1945.

After arriving in New York, James received a delay en route to his next base, which gave him a leave to visit home. After nineteen days at home, he went to his assigned base at Santa Ana, California. It was a convalescent base. He spent three months there and then was reassigned to Scott Field, Illinois, the same place James took his radio training. There he worked in the maintenance shop and was discharged on

October 8, 1945. James says, "It was quite an experience for an eighteen-year-old kid. God was with me and my crew all through these missions."

James Debth returned home, worked at the Jeep plant for a while, and then went to work at the Toledo, Ohio, post office. After thirty-five years, he retired, and he and his wife moved to Temperance, Michigan. His wife has since passed away.

It was a precious gift for Raymond Miller to meet Allen Hamman, James Debth, and Arthur Lovrien thanks to son-in-law, Lee Moorman. Lee Moorman had been visiting Wright Patterson Air Field and met a comrade who had served in the 452nd Group in World War II with Raymond. He made it a mission for Raymond to meet Colonel Allen Hamman and the crewmen who were on the aircraft when Raymond was injured. The meeting, Raymond says, "might be described as coincidental but I call it providence." Raymond's son-in-law, Lee Moorman, is a Bronze Star Vietnam veteran.

Chapter 19

God's Blessings

Raymond now resides at the Lafayette, Indiana, Veterans' Home where he keeps active. He is a person who displays his core of love with a calming acceptance that draws one in. Values and experiences seemed to have shaped his life with a strong living faith.

He gives presentations there at the facility and numerous other locations where he has been invited to speak. He enjoys people and is a mentoring type. He travels and speaks at libraries, schools, firefighters' organizations and the Purdue Officers' Club and recently spoke to a group of Hamilton County Veterans (Corp/Navy) at Noblesville, Indiana, where he was given a life membership. He will go wherever asked. He helps the Veterans' Home Chaplain by greeting, handing out information, and serving in the convocation on Sunday morning. He mentors a young thirteen-year-old girl, daughter of a staff worker at the veterans' facility. On Sunday morning, during the chapel service, she sits beside Raymond. He gives her Bible assignments to study, and then they will discuss it together. They share a very special bond—much like an adopted-granddaughter-and-grandfather relationship. While practice teaching, Raymond would tutor a young child to help them with a subject. I don't believe *no* is in Raymond Miller's vocabulary.

Raymond goes to all the veteran memorial services of those who pass away at the Veteran's Home *if* he is able to attend. In December 2012, Raymond helped to lay wreaths on the veterans' graves at the Veteran's Home Cemetery. Raymond's openness and humanitarian engagements of love he has for others speaks volumes for the kind of person he is.

The veterans' home is just a few miles from his beloved Purdue University. It was where his war years had started, and it is like returning home for Raymond. After seventy years, ninety-year-old Raymond Miller, a Purdue baseball catcher in 1942, joined a Purdue team for the day. The final week of the 2013 season, Coach Doug Schreiber welcomed Raymond to the field to throw out the ceremonial first pitch for Purdue's home game versus Iowa. It had been an age-old dream of Raymond's to play baseball at Purdue. He visited the new Alexander Field facilities (named after Purdue's former coach Dave Alexander). Raymond shook hands with the players and spoke to the players of his Purdue and military experiences. Raymond got to see the locker room that brought back *special* memories.

Raymond Miller was called up for active duty before the spring games, so he never got to take to the field to play for Coach Fehring and the Boilermaker baseball nine. "The day was an experience of my life," says Raymond Miller. "I was so deeply honored. It brought back so many memories that I had years ago. Purdue is like a second home to me, so that's how I felt and am deeply grateful for my dream to be fulfilled."

In 2012, Raymond had the honor of going to Washington DC on a World War II tribute journey on a veterans' honor flight to visit the National World War II Memorial. It was a trip of a lifetime with many thanks to the Greater Lafayette, Indiana, Honor Flight Committee: Mayor Tony Roswarski, Copresident (Gold Star Mothers) Pam Mow, Copresident Dana Vann, Marilyn Frantz, and Brenda Wilson along with the eight board members at large. There were eighty-four veterans on the flight, with guardians. Raymond was accompanied by Chris Turpin as a guardian for the day. Chris has become a *special* person in Raymond's life since the Washington trip.

Raymond Miller took part in the B-17G Flying Fortress *Aluminum Overcast* show at Purdue University on August 9-11, 2013. For Raymond, it was a step back in time to his World War II copilot days flying the "Great Machine." Many came for the aviation history, to see one of the vital aircraft during World War II. In addition to a few World War II veterans, sons or grandchildren also shared the B-17 memories of their fathers and grandfathers who flew, served, and sacrificed on the Flying Fortress aircraft. It was a very memorable time for history enthusiasts. The *Aluminum Overcast* is a traveling museum, flying to keep the record of the B-17 history intact.

Raymond got to fly in the B-17G Flying Fortress *Aluminum Overcast,* which was like what he had flown during combat missions over France and Germany. To fly once again in a beloved B-17G aircraft was such an honor. Raymond got to fly, sitting right behind where he once sat as copilot, thanks to pilot Rick Fernalld and copilot Ken Morris. Both made the flight for Raymond a memorable one.

Rick Fernalld flew B-52s from 1972 until 1977. He flew a tour in Guam and one in Thailand, supporting air operations in Southeast Asia. His home base was Mather AFB, Sacramento County, California. He served in the 441st Bomb Squadron and the 320th Bomb Wing.

Ken Morris flew for both Delta and Northwest airlines. He has flown 725, 727, DC-9, and Boeing 757/767 aircraft. Ken has three thousand flight hours with Beechcraft Model 18 or *Twin Beech* airplane as it is better known. He learned to fly a Cessna 140 single-engine two-seater airplane at age sixteen and has flown ever since.

Ken Morris is owner of *Taildragger Aviation* business located in Northern Illinois, on the Poplar Grove Airport (C77). Ken's wife, Lorraine, does interiors on Cessna 120s, 140s, and 140As as well as other airplanes, and they also do complete restorations. Ken isn't the only pilot in the family, his wife, Lorraine, is a pilot for United Airlines. Next year, Ken will check out as captain to left seat.

Ken also ferries all kinds of airplanes all over the United States, from J-3 Cubs, Stearmans, Beech 18s, and DC-3s. The three days at Purdue, Rick and Ken along with the crew members contributed so much to make the *Aluminum Overcast* show a memorable one for those that attended.

Aboard the *Aluminum Overcast* was a young mechanic who, during World War II, would have been an older man. Mike Peer graduated from high school in 2008 and started at Fox Valley Technical College (FVTC), in Oshkosh, Wisconsin, the following fall. He enrolled in the airframe and powerplant mechanics program. While attending FVTC, he also volunteered at the EAA's Weeks Hangar. He then stayed an additional year at FVTC and completed his associate's degree in aircraft electronics. Immediately after graduation (June 2011) Mike began working full-time for the Experimental Aircraft Association and has been there just over two years full-time. Mike now is enrolled at the University of Wisconsin-Oshkosh pursing a bachelor's degree in aviation management with a plan to obtain his inspection authorization as well as additional flight ratings. His career goal is to fly warbirds and advance to a director of maintenance and/or a flying position.

The gross weight of sixty-five thousand pounds the B-17 carried during World War II bombing missions made the ship much harder to control and for a much longer takeoff run than the *Aluminum Overcast* flight on August 9, 2013. Raymond spent three days at the Purdue University Airport, Lafayette, Indiana, welcoming visitors. It was so inspiring how Raymond encompassed his pilot's experiences and B-17 history that are forever planted in memory. For the event, Raymond was contacted by the Experimental Aviation Association (EAA) president, John Cox, who hosted the historical event. The B-17 was on a national tour. For Raymond, it was a joyful three days.

The *Aluminum Overcast* aircraft arrived too late in May 1945 to see combat missions in World War II. It served as a cargo hauler, an aerial mapping platform, and in forest dusting and pest control applications. There are ten B-17G model aircraft that are still airworthy today. Along with well-known *Aluminum Overcast* are *Memphis Belle*, *Nine-O-Nine*, *Sentimental Journey*, *Texas Raiders*, *Yankee Lady*, *Fuddy Duddy*, *Evergreen International*, *Miss Angela*, and *Thunderbird*. Several are in museums, and two are under restoration for airworthiness. France has *Pink Lady* (airworthy) and one under restoration; United Kingdom has one airworthy, two in museums; and Brazil has one on display and one under restoration.

Raymond Miller keeps in contact with Harold "Hal" Kristal. They are the only surviving members of their B-17 crew that they know of. Hal and his wife live in sunny Oceanside, California, and he says he wouldn't want to live anywhere else. He enjoys the weather having lived in Minnesota.

Raymond and Hal say that they have been blessed. They had witnessed equal measures of courage and terror. They both gave purely; with that, the honor came in giving and duty. That was honor enough for Raymond and Hal. Now they have their memories of their beloved B-17G Flying Fortress silhouetted against the sky with peace. For Raymond and Hal, love is not only in word but also deed. They gave for the love of country.

Raymond feels honored to have two children named after him shared with pilot, Harry Simmons. His flight crew pilot and copilot, Lynn Davis, would name his son *Harry Raymond*. Davis's daughter, Pam, named a son *Harry Raymond* after her brother. Pam's son, Russell, is a World War II buff since his early elementary years of school. He served twenty years with the Coast Guard Reserves and went three years at the Coast Guard Academy in New London, Connecticut. Russell, a firefighter, joined the 728th Airlift Squadron, a United States Air Force Reserve Squadron. It is a corollary unit of the active duty Eighth Airlift Squadron located at McChord Air Force Base, Washington. It is part of the 446th Airlift wing and operates the C-17 Globemaster III transport aircraft.

Russell's grandfather, Lynn Davis, served with the 728th Squadron as a flight engineer on the B-17 Flying Fortress in Europe during World War II. The 728th's mission is to provide mission-ready airlifts for operational support for strategic and tactical airlift, combat airlift, and aeromedical evacuation in support of United States Air Force Reserves' command. On August 12, 2013, Russell was sworn into his grandfather's old 728th Squadron in the air force. Russell says, "I can serve twenty years with the 728th Airlift Squadron Reserves."

1st Lt. Raymond Miller Pilot

Russell Holmes posted on Facebook, August 12, 2013:

> Don't post often but today was kind for me. After 2 years of waiting for an opening, I finally was successful in one of my major goals. After long and rewarding career in the Coast Guard since 1986, I have switched things up a bit and reenlisted in the Air Force Reserves.
>
> The best part is that I will be joining the 728th Airlift Squadron which is the squadron that my grandfather was a member of flying on B-17's out of England in WW2. I'll be training for a loadmaster position on a C-17 in the near future and am incredibly excited. Can't wait to start drilling again!

Lynn Davis, a twenty-year veteran of the air force during World War II, flew thirty-four missions over Europe. He stayed in the reserves and was recalled for the Korean War and flew missions as a tail gunner on B-29s. The B-29 strategic bomber was known as the most powerful, most destructive weapon of World War II. Lynn Davis remained in the service and later served on B-36s and the more powerful B-52 strategic bombers, a modified version of the Super Fortress that the air force used in every theater of World War II and across four decades. Lynn Davis retired January 1970 from the air force. Lynn died in 1990. Raymond Miller's friend was sixty-six.

Young waist gunner Donald Sutter, who trained and went overseas with Harry and Raymond's crew early on, was assigned to another crew. Along with his waist gunner duties he would turn on a gadget (signal of direction) to dazzle the radio signal the enemy received. Captain Sutter would earn rank of first lieutenant by war's end. He returned home and became a successful banker in California. He passed away about six years ago.

Raymond with mother, Josephine "Josie" Miller, Ray is dressed in his "pinks and greens" officer's service uniform, 1945.

Raymond on the patio.

1st Lt. Raymond Miller Pilot

Raymond (a very good golfer) with his golf clubs, 1945.

Raymond with his baseball bat.

Raymond with his Gas City OnIzers basketball team. Left to right, standing, are Dan Foreman (manager), Max Denton, Jake Adrianson Jr., John Rhoday Jr., Melvin Huffman, and Everett Dalton. In the front row, left to right, are Gene Estle, Wendell Detamore, Joe Bothwell, and Raymond Miller, 1946.

Raymond Miller when he graduated from Ohio State College in 1951.

1st Lt. Raymond Miller Pilot

Left and right are Raymond Miller and Jack Evans at the B-17 *Yankee Lady* Air Show, Marion, Indiana.

L-R: Mark Miller, son of Raymond Miller.

Mark and wife Linda Miller.

L-R: Raymond Miller and George Culnon. Raymond Miller and daughter, Linda, visited George at his home in Wilton, West Virginia.

1st Lt. Raymond Miller Pilot

L-R: Raymond Miller with son-in-law, Lee Moorman, at the 452nd Group reunion held in Council Bluffs, Iowa.

L-R: Raymond Miller and daughter, Linda, at the 452nd Group Reunion.

L-R: Raymond Miller meeting with pilot, Col. Allen Hamman, for the first time since November 5, 1944.

L-R: Col. Allen Hamman, Art Lovrien, and Raymond Miller.

1st Lt. Raymond Miller Pilot

L-R: Step-grandson, Tyler Romine, Raymond Miller, and stepson, Dr. Richard Romine, at Wrigley Field visiting a Cubs baseball game in Chicago, Illinois.

L-R: Raymond and wife, Alma Miller.

Raymond Miller at the Indiana Veterans' Home in 2011, giving a presentation.

L-R: Bailey Keller and Raymond Miller. Picture courtesy of David Fraley.

1st Lt. Raymond Miller Pilot

Raymond out at the Veterans' Home cemetery. Picture courtesy of David Fraley.

L-R: Raymond Miller and Christine "Chris" Turpin at an Honor Flight meeting to visit the National World War II Memorial on a veteran's World War II tribute journey to Washington DC, April 2012.

L-R: Dana Vann, Raymond Miller, Chris Turpin, and Purdue coach Doug Schreiber at the final week of the 2013 season of Purdue vs. Iowa baseball game.

L-R: Raymond Miller (Purdue baseball catcher in 1942) and Dana Vann. After seventy years, Coach Schreiber welcomed Raymond to the field to throw out the ceremonial first pitch for the Purdue's Home game versus Iowa. An age-old dream of Raymond's was to play baseball at Purdue University.

1st Lt. Raymond Miller Pilot

Picture of Raymond Miller that Rick Fernalld took during a video interview after returning from an *Aluminum Overcast* Flight

L-R, standing: Copilot Ken Morris, pilot Rick Fernalld, and Raymond Miller seated. In the background, a young man from the Lafayette TV station is getting ready to interview Raymond.

L-R: Raymond Miller and Mike Peer (EAA mechanic).

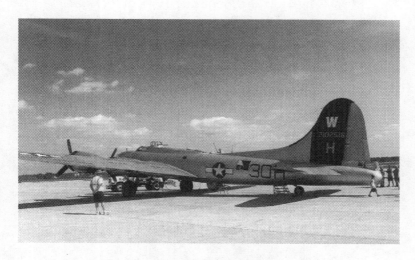

Picture of B-17G Flying Fortress *Aluminum Overcast* aircraft at Purdue, August 9-11, 2013. Raymond Miller was contacted by Experimental Aviation Association (EAA) president, John Cox, who hosted the historical event. The B-17 was on a nationwide tour.

1st Lt. Raymond Miller Pilot

L-R: Ruby Gwin (author) and Raymond Miller on August 9, 2013, at the B-17, Purdue University Airport. Raymond says, "This airplane was like an old mother hen. See the big, broad wings. It gave us a sense of protection."

Russell Homes in his swearing-in to the 728th Airlift Squadron, of which was the squadron that his grandfather was a member flying on B-17's out of England in World War II

This picture of Raymond Miller is so unique. Raymond is a humble man with words of vision and wisdom—sincere and direct, expressing clearly and with emphasis—a modest man with a *twinkle* in his eye of a *caring* and *happy* man. This beautiful picture was taken by photographer David Fraley on March 30, 2013. It was Raymond and David's first meeting. Mr. Fraley, Historian, was former "Interim Executive Director" at The Carter House, Franklin, Tennessee.

1st Lt. Raymond Miller Pilot

Raymond displays a core of love with a calming acceptance that draws one in. Values and experiences seemed to have shaped his life with a strong living faith. One can say, as the apostle Paul, Raymond's life is characterized by love, compassion, focus, and countless other noble qualities. Raymond has a significant impact on those whom he meets.

In 1945, Raymond returned to *life as a civilian,* having known fear and courage on a foreign land far from home. With his nine-member crew, they made an enviable record of which they could be most proud. All individuals displayed fine spirit and efficiency in carrying out their missions in spite of difficult times. Each crew member would return home at mission's end safely or stay in the air force for new challenges—all with great courage.

"God gave me the tools to have depth perception with the ability to perform and eyesight to do my job," says Raymond. "I had never expected to return home. To our country, for the many sacrifices given during World War II, in humble gratitude, I thank them."

Our *home front* gave an overwhelming superiority by staying united in the war efforts in order to help win the war and placed at our country's disposal great reserves of well-trained fighting men who were proud to serve the Allied Expedition Forces. Our homelands' loyalty and indomitable courage in the face of all but insuperable obstacles and their unselfish cooperation in all areas helped the victory. To those who made the history chronicled herein and the heroes who never came home and those who lie mutely in American cemeteries on foreign lands and at home, they shall never be forgotten.

My Dreams

I have lived my Air Corps pilot dreams
And see them in visions,
Where long they will cling to me.
I have lived my old glory-flying dreams
And served them with wisdom,
Where long they will live in me.

Ruby Gwin and Raymond Miller

Chapter 20

Raymond's Log Sheet/452nd Statistics

Raymond Miller	Log Sheet		A/C Serial #	A/C Disposition	Time
11/04/1944	Neunkirchen	Saturday	43-37673	*That's All Jack*	6:15
11/05/1944	Ludwigshafen	Sunday	43-37673	*That's All Jack*	6:00
12/24/1944	Darmstadt	Sunday	43-38822	unknown	8:30
12/26/1944	Andernach	Tuesday	44-8527	*Sweet Stuff*	5:15
12/28/1944	Koblenz	Thursday	44-8531	*Miassis Dragon*	6:05
1/2/1945	Ehrang	Tuesday	43-37542	*Smokey Liz II*	6:15
1/3/1945	Fulda	Wednesday	42-107073	*Silver Shed House*	9:05
1/8/1945	Lünebach-Waxweiler	Monday	44-8527	*Sweet Stuff*	7:15
1/10/1945	Cologne	Wednesday	43-37802	unknown	5:45
1/17/1945	Hamburg	Wednesday	44-8527	*Sweet Stuff*	7:00
1/20/1945	Rheine	Saturday	44-8527	*Sweet Stuff*	5:35
1/21/1945	Mannheim	Sunday	44-8527	*Sweet Stuff*	7:30
2/22/1945	Freiburg-Ulm	Thursday	43-38982	*Warzend*	8:00
2/23/1945	Ansbach	Friday	43-38982	*Warzend*	8:00

2/25/1945	Munich	Sunday	43-38982	*Warzend*	9:00
3/1/1945	Ulm	Thursday	43-38982	*Warzend*	8:35
3/5/1945	Chemnitz	Monday	43-38982	*Warzend*	8:30
3/8/1945	Langendreer	Thursday	43-38982	*Warzend*	7:00
3/10/1945	Dortmund	Saturday	43-38982	*Warzend*	6:15
3/11/1945	Hamburg	Sunday	43-38982	*Warzend*	6:10
3/14/1945	Hanover	Wednesday	43-38876	unknown	5:50
3/15/1945	Oranienburg	Thursday	43-388982	*Warzend*	7:20

452nd Statistics
250 missions
7, 275 sorties
450 KIA
110 MIA
200 B-17s lost

Army Air Forces statistics. There were 94,565 American air combat casualties with 30,099 killed in action. 51,106 American airmen were missing in action, POWs, evaders, or internees.

Awards. Purple Heart, Presidential Unit Citation, Air Medal with two Bronze Oak Leaf Clusters, American Campaign Medal, European-African-Middle Eastern Campaign Medal with three Bronze Service Stars, World War II Victory Medal, Pilot Wings, Honorable Lapel Button-World War II.

Campaigns. Air defense, Northern France, Rhineland, Ardennes-Alsace, Central Europe.

Raymond Miller's total flight hours: 642—combat: 180

About the Author

Ruby Gwin was born and raised in rural Indiana, married and mother of three children. As a history buff, she has penned and copyrighted nine books of which this will be her fifth release. You can visit her at www.rubygwin.com.